CITIZEN MUCKRAKING

How To Investigate and
Right Wrongs In Your Community

The Center for Public Integrity

Common Courage Media   Monroe, ME

**Library of Congress Cataloging-in-Publication Data
is available from the publisher.**

Common Courage Media
Box 702
Monroe, ME 04951

(207) 525-0900 fax: (207) 525-3068
orders-info@commoncouragepress.com

www.commoncouragepress.com

First Printing

Contents

Chapter Three
State Secrets

Chapter Four
Local Heroes

Chapter Five
Giving Corporations the Business

Contents

Chapter Six
Environmental Forces

Chapter Seven
Consumer Protection

Chapter Eight
Opposition Research

Chapter Nine
Brave New Worlds

Chapter Ten
Spreading the Message

Foreword

With 6 billion people on the planet and 275 million living in the United States, who can blame anyone for thinking that one person can't make a difference? But don't believe it for a second.

Citizen Muckraking contains inspiring stories about ordinary people who started asking basic questions about things in their communities that somehow just didn't seem right. They wrote letters, attended hearings, obtained government documents, asked direct questions of public officials—all things that full-time, professional investigative reporters do day in and day out—and their questions actually brought about change. In other words, the truth emerged, the public became enraged, and wrongs were righted.

This book outlines some basic techniques that you—or any other citizen—can use to obtain information about the toxic-waste dump in your neighborhood; the city-council zoning decision that seems to benefit one of the council members personally; the reason your utility rates have been going up; why some property-tax assessments increase yearly but others don't; etc. Information truly is power, and we will show you precisely how to get the facts.

In two decades as an investigative journalist, uncovering impropriety around the nation and abroad, countless times I have seen individuals persistently ask unpopular but entirely reasonable questions about matters affecting their daily lives: the air they breathe, the water they drink, the food they buy and eat, the schools their children attend. And frequently their curiosity and perseverance have brought about change that improves the quality of those same lives.

In my eleven years at ABC News and CBS News, most recently as a producer for Mike Wallace at the program 60 *Minutes*, there was no single story I investigated that was more inspiring to me than the one titled "The Czar of Clinton County." At the show's offices in New York City, we received a letter from a citizen living in Albany, Kentucky, containing the plaintive cry: "Please come. We need your help." 60 *Minutes* gets thousands of letters a year, but for many reasons this one stood out to me. Within days I was on a plane to Kentucky, flying into Louisville, and driving three hours south into the heart of rural Appalachia, into one of the nation's very poorest counties, where the median per-capita income was less than $5,000. Many of the 9,300 people living in the county eked out their livings on the land, raising livestock, farming, and working in a few factories.

But the biggest employer by far was the school system, which received 90 percent or more of its money from the federal and state governments. The superintendent of schools, Robert Polston, was easily the most powerful man in the area. He ruled the county. The Polston-run school system represented perhaps the worst public-school education in the United States: Kentucky was ranked dead last in education among the 50 states, and Clinton County had the lowest test scores in all of Kentucky. At the time we came onto the scene, the *Louisville Courier-Journal* had published some enterprising stories about the corruption and fraud in Clinton County, and the U.S. Department of Education and the FBI were conducting ongoing investigations into allegations ranging from misappropriation of funds to forgery of government documents, voter fraud, and payroll padding.

Local citizens—led by a remarkable, courageous woman named Martha Marcum, minister Ernest Harris, attorney Elmer Heist, and others—had started asking uncomfortable questions about the board of education's records and the funding of the various school programs, among other things, and found they were unable to get any answers. To gain clout and credibility, they formed an organization called Citizens for Better Education in Clinton County. But they were still terribly isolated, socially and politically. Worse, they were being penalized for merely asking questions: Relatives working in the school system as custodians or substitute teachers were fired. As a dire situation became more desperate, the citizens of Clinton County alerted the news media, first the *Louisville Courier-Journal* and then *60 Minutes*.

What I will never forget, though, was the raw fear. Everyone was terrified of Polston, his family, and his cronies. When I first entered the city limits of county seat Albany in my rental car bearing Jefferson County (Louisville) license plates, literally within minutes I found myself being followed. Trees and houses seemed to have eyes in this very, very small town. I met with brave teachers behind a cemetery after midnight and made sure not to park my suddenly well-known car anywhere near their houses. These anonymous whistleblowers were worried about losing their jobs, of course, but they also feared for their physical safety and mine, offering me a "piece," which I quickly realized was a handgun. I informed them that I might shoot off my own foot with that thing, but I thanked them for their concern. As we met, cars kept circling the area, trying to ascertain where I was and with whom I was meeting.

After we investigated the school system for weeks, it was time to bring in Mike Wallace and two camera crews. There was no hotel or motel in the county that could accommodate us, so we had to secure lodging in the next county. As Wallace, producer Lowell Bergman, and I were sitting down to dinner the night before filming was to begin, a gentleman came over, introduced himself, and asked if we would please accompany him. Curious and having no idea what was up, we followed him to a private room in the back of the restaurant. There, behind closed doors, sat about two dozen citizens of Clinton County—none of whom I had ever met, seen, or interviewed. They had heard we were coming to town, ascertained where we were staying, and driven more than 20 miles to meet secretly with us.

That night they told us harrowing tales: of unprosecuted, unreported sexual assault; of unsolved arson against people not "with the program"; of federal taxpayer money designated for teaching handicapped children instead being pocketed, with the parents of those children being told to keep their disabled children at home because there was "no money" to educate them. We learned more about how Superintendent Robert Polston had 23 relatives on the school-system payroll, including teachers and principals, even though some of them I'd met seemed, frankly, dumber than a post. They told us of astonishingly poor-quality instruction in schools, of retaliation against the slightest dissent by anyone, and of a rubber-stamp board of education handpicked by Polston and ratified by the traumatized voters. It was all quite emotional and unforgettable, and several people broke down and cried. Mike Wallace, who had done hundreds of 60 *Minutes* stories all over the world, was clearly taken aback.

That night in our hotel rooms, we were visited by the Kentucky State Police, who advised us to leave because they had received a threat against our lives. But at that point, there was no way we were leaving.

The next day, with our convoy of vehicles and film equipment, we drove into tiny Albany, Kentucky. We wanted to film the monthly school-board meeting, which was required by state law to be open to the public, including the news media. The Clinton County Board of Education held its monthly meetings in a house, in a room that could comfortably seat only about 25 people at most.

Martha Marcum and the other concerned citizens showed up and sat up in front. They directly faced Polston, a large man who enjoyed smoking large cigars, and the members of the school board. The superintendent proposed a few things, and the board members mumbled their assent, sitting there virtually motionless. None of them said more than "Yea." With the cameras on, Mike Wallace turned the meeting into an interrogation of the grandest, most overdue kind, asking the board members why they never asked a single question. Wallace asked Odell Gross, the chairman of the school board, "Over the years, have you or the other school-board members looked at the files, looked at the financial books?"

"No, sir," Gross said.

"Why not?" Wallace asked.

"It's just something that's never been done since I've been on the board 32 years."

When Wallace started asking Polston—who had declined our request for an interview—direct questions about all of his relatives

4

on the payroll, the burly superintendent's face turned red, he was sweating, and he literally began to chew on his tie. It was unbelievable, and all captured for posterity on film. Polston complained that no one had ever asked him such questions, and it showed.

At one point, Polston tried to suggest that all of the allegations against him and his stewardship of the school system were "just politics." That explanation triggered an eloquent rage in Martha Marcum.

"I hate politics," she said, "but I realize that good people have got to get involved in politics because evil flourishes when good people sit and do nothing."

Martha Marcum epitomizes what we are talking about in *Citizen Muckraking*: People who have become frustrated with their government, their local businesses, and other institutions seek answers and often get them—and in the process their energy and insistence provoke discourse and, ultimately, progress.

Within weeks of our broadcast of the Clinton County story, Robert Polston was forced to resign his position as superintendent of schools.

I subsequently left *60 Minutes* and founded The Center for Public Integrity, a nonprofit, nonpartisan research organization based in Washington, D.C. The Center is staffed by expatriate investigative journalists from the nation's leading newspapers, magazines, and television networks, who want to get straight answers to questions that affect our lives and our democracy. We work without the normal time and space limitations that most journalists operate under.

In over 40 reports and books since 1990, the Center has investigated and exposed, on behalf of the American people, all kinds of fraud, mismanagement, and corruption. Just as many ordinary folks have done in their local communities, after doing some research we have also confronted our politicians, asking such simple questions as: Is it true that 110 members of Congress used more than $10 million in leftover campaign funds for their own personal use? (Yes.) Did *half* of the White House trade officials over a fifteen-year period, upon leaving government, go to work for foreign governments and foreign corporations? (Yes.) Even though the job of political party chairman is a full-time position, is it true that half of the party chairmen from 1977 to 1992 had conflicts of interest because they derived income, usually law-firm retainer fees, from helping out certain corporations with business before the government? (Yes.) Did health-care-industry interests ply members of Congress with 181 all-expenses-paid trips and $30 million in campaign contributions, and hire more than 80 former members, their staff, and other government officials, just before Congress killed health-care reform in 1994? (Yes.)

In 1996, we decided that it was time for the American people to look on presidential candidates as their prospective employees. Thus, as a means of providing voters with employee background information, we wrote a popular, investigative book, *The Buying of the President* (Avon), the first exposé to examine the special interests behind the presidential candidates. It was released a month before the Iowa caucuses. Later in the presidential election year, we put together a list of 75 wealthy donors to the Democratic Party who had slept over in the Clinton White House. That issue of our newsletter, *The Public i*, titled "Fat Cat Hotel," effectively broke the Clinton White House "Lincoln Bedroom" scandal. The investigation was subsequently given the Society of Professional Journalists' 1996 Public Service in Newsletter Journalism Award.

I could recount many other questions we have had about our public officials, their conduct and policy decisions, and the remarkable truths that ultimately emerged after we found out the answers. The point is that what we have been doing at The Center for Public Integrity can be—and is being—replicated all over the nation. Indeed, our Web site (www.publicintegrity.org) has a special section that showcases some of the most inspiring cases of citizen muckraking in the United States, and also provides an interactive forum for questions from people around the country who are trying to dig out information. (If you don't have access to the Internet, write or call the Center at 910 17th Street, NW, 7th Floor, Washington, D.C. 20006; 202-466-1300.)

Just as it's wise to live by the Latin phrase *caveat emptor* when we buy a toaster, a car, or a house, we should be similarly vigilant when it comes to decisions that the government, companies, labor unions, charities, churches, and other institutions make that affect our lives.

Foreword

First, we must be aware of what has been decided, and if it seems to favor one interest or clique unfairly over everyone else, then it's time for a little sunshine in this democracy of ours. This book is meant to empower you in your quest for truth, justice, and the American way.

Charles Lewis
Washington, D.C.
January 2000

Introduction

Y ou can indeed fight city hall. And just about anyone else, for that matter.

Linda Price King is proof of that. The founder and executive director of the Virginia-based Environmental Health Network was lured into the role of eco-activist only after witnessing firsthand the health effects of hazardous wastes. While her neighbors brooded privately about the environmental devastation going on around them, King decided to take her fight public. It's a battle her opponents won't soon forget.

King's unlikely road to civic activism started in Nitro, West Virginia. Drive west on Interstate 64 from Charleston, the Mountaineer State's quaint, riverside capital, and in twenty minutes you'll come upon the imposing smokestacks and fouled air of Nitro. At night, the small town has the eerie feel of a *Mad Max* movie set, as great, billowy plumes are pumped skyward from cavernous factories aglow with activity. The odor can be overwhelming, and the typical reaction of unsuspecting motorists is to keep on driving, straight for the Kentucky line.

But not everyone simply passes Nitro by. People live there. They work in those factories, and their children attend school in the shadow of those smokestacks. That may be hard for visitors to imagine, but even more improbable is this: Things used to be a lot worse.

Introduction

Linda King knows that. She and her former husband moved to Nitro in the early 1980s, unaware that this part of West Virginia—and her adopted hometown in particular—was a toxic dump, an industrial enclave whose unusually high level of the carcinogenic chemical dioxin helped earn it the nickname "Cancer Valley." A real-estate agent took the young couple into town the back way, to obscure views of the incinerators and chemical plants. The deal was done quickly, and for just $29,000 the Kings had themselves a place to build their future and raise a family. Linda King was surprised by the low price of her house but didn't question it further. Instead, she settled in for a life that she describes as "Ms. Betty Crocker."

But the idyllic existence was short-lived. Her children became ill, and she developed an immune-deficiency disease that ultimately kept her from working. In her neighborhood of some two dozen homes, seven people had cancer and others were diagnosed with muscular dystrophy or lupus. The paws of family pets would bleed for no apparent reason. Lung disease was prevalent in the community. In fact, doctors described the lungs of nonsmokers there as comparable to those who had smoked heavily throughout their lives.

It was no wonder: Nitro was home to six specialty chemical companies as well as a hazardous-waste incinerator. The sky was often filled with multicolored streaks. Experimental pesticides were being illegally dumped. Playgrounds were built over discarded barrels of unknown chemicals. King would later look back on her adopted hometown as "a chemical holocaust."

Disturbed by the mysterious odors, she finally went door to door in search of answers. What she learned from neighbors stunned her: The situation in their town had actually improved over the last two decades. Longtime residents recounted how white house paint actually used to blacken when blanketed by factory emissions.

Others may have been resigned to this fate, but not King. She initiated community surveys in hopes of tracking the number of affected residents and the onset of symptoms. She lobbied state agencies—often futilely—for assistance. She dug up documents in the state capital, piecing together lists of chemicals being released into the air or trucked to the dumps. She asked chemical-company representatives to her home for explanations. And with a small band of neighbors, a group that called themselves Concerned Citizens of Nitro, she instituted what the local newspapers dubbed "nose patrols"—early-morning forays along town roads to track the smell of chemicals to their sources. Plant managers were then roused from bed and invited to experience this pollution for themselves.

King's battle paid dividends. Illegal dumping in the town was curbed, as was the release of toxins. Local companies became more responsive to citizens' concerns. The West Virginia Pollution Control Commission became more stringent in its regulation of Nitro's companies. This parcel of West Virginia was by no means transferred into the "almost heaven" that John Denver sang about in "Country Roads," but the trend nonetheless became positive.

As for King, the health effects of living in this environment proved too much, and she was forced to move. But she didn't give up the fight. In fact, she took the knowledge gained from her Nitro experiences and used it to help other citizens' groups investigate the threat of chemical exposure. The Environmental Health Network was born from these efforts, and the organization became an effective catalyst for reform on the federal, state, and local levels. For an encore, King recently authored a valuable guide to chemical-injury litigation.

Of course, Linda King is not entirely unique. From coast to coast, individuals and community groups are having increasing success in their battles with unresponsive corporations and public officials. By blending activism with grassroots organizing and old-fashioned investigative reporting, citizens are discovering that they're not so easily thwarted by those in power.

Such activism has been spurred, in part, by a frustration with the status quo. Public-opinion polls show, for example, that only four in ten Americans believe they have a say in how things are run in the United States. More strikingly, nearly three-quarters of us believe that ordinary people don't have much of a say because the experts wield all the power. Couple these findings with another—that fewer and fewer Americans believe their government will usually do the right thing—and it's not hard to understand why citizen participation in our democracy is waning.

At the same time, however, a growing number of people who feel disempowered and disenfranchised are taking matters into their own hands. Taking a page from Linda King's activist manifesto, these otherwise ordinary citizens are tackling community problems by getting involved.

"People have given up on capital-P politics," says the overseer of a community-service grant program in North Carolina. "They're trying to do the work they can see, where they know they can make a difference."

In one Illinois community, an activist's research resulted in nontoxic chemicals being substituted for toxic ones in a mosquito-abatement program—a program later copied statewide. In Nebraska, a citizens' group used the Freedom of Information Act to unearth files showing that state officials were failing to keep a major meatpacking plant from polluting the Missouri River. In Maryland, community activists unearthed documents to prove their suspicions that politically connected developers were receiving a sweetheart deal from state highway officials. In Washington, D.C., organizations that previously brought constituents to the nation's capital to lobby legislators have successfully used the Internet and e-mail campaigns to achieve the same results.

"This is the equivalent of a nonviolent revolution, and it's not very well known," says Franklin Thomas, former president of the Ford Foundation, a philanthropy based in New York City. "It's people in communities and neighborhoods organizing to cause positive things to happen, feeling the sense of responsibility and becoming totally subject to the policy whims of any level of government."

Although their causes may be different, one trait these activists share is their use of investigative reporting techniques. Many never realized that they were in fact being investigative reporters, but they nonetheless became proficient in using those time-honored methods—whether searching land records, investigating politicians, scrutinizing law-enforcement files, following paper trails, unearthing background information on companies and private individuals, or, ultimately, informing the public of their findings.

But not everyone is proficient in those techniques. Not everyone knows where to look for information about licensed professionals, for example, or which publicly accessible databases will save them days, perhaps weeks, of library research. Few would-be muckrakers know the legalities of sifting through trash or where to find financial information that corporations try to keep from public view.

Citizen Muckraking will help fill in these gaps. It will help you learn the techniques of investigative reporting and apply them to issues of interest in your own community. It shows how grassroots organizations have approached their local battles, and it augments these experiences with tips and insight from the experts. Finally, *Citizen Muckraking* provides a road map for reaching a goal that is often elusive but is every citizen's right: holding officials and institutions accountable for their actions.

CHAPTER ONE

The Freedom of Information Act

The Freedom of Information Act can turn seemingly futile investigations into fruitful ones. But unless you know the secrets to using it effectively, your search for documents may bear little but disappointment.

Take Interstate 10 across Mobile Bay and, on a clear night, you may see the lights in Fairhope, eight miles south. They won't be bright—just flickers emanating from a thousand-foot, concrete pier that's a landmark in this out-of-the-way patch of southern Alabama. As residents will tell you, Fairhope is quintessential small-town America: Crime isn't much of an issue. Main Street, with its refurbished old buildings, is a throwback to an era that the residents of other places only reminisce about. When a decision was made to build a playground and park a few years ago, half the townspeople volunteered their labor or supplies.

Ron Hayes is one of Fairhope's 10,000 inhabitants. Born and raised in Birmingham, Hayes later moved to Mobile, then continued his southerly migration to Fairhope, where he and his wife, Dot, raised their family. He seems like the right sort of person for a place like this. Friendly, polite, and soft-spoken, he has the demeanor of someone who'd rather turn the other cheek than embroil himself in confrontation. But Ron Hayes has another side—a fearsome tenacity that's enough to send even the worthiest opponent in search of a white flag.

Just ask officials of the federal Occupational Safety and Health Administration, who since 1993 have had to endure Hayes's relentless quest for documents. "I called OSHA once a week for two years," he says. "At first they wouldn't speak to me; I had to leave messages. After a year they got tired of that and started talking to me. Sometimes, though, they wouldn't talk to me, but they knew I called: I made the receptionist give me their voicemail. That's the kind of persistence I used."

Hayes's persistence has yielded a four-foot stack of paper—a long leap from the 52 pages that OSHA sent in reply to his initial request for documents. And it's persistence that will no doubt push the pile higher, because as Hayes will tell you, he's just getting warmed up.

To understand Ron Hayes's obsession, you need to go back to De Funiak Springs on October 22, 1993. The largest employer in this small Florida Panhandle town was Showell Farms, a poultry processor that in January 1995 was purchased by Perdue Farms. Among the company's workforce that day was Ron's nineteen-year-old son, Patrick, who had relocated to De Funiak Springs two and a half months earlier and whose distaste for his grueling, $5-an-hour job had already set in motion his plans to return to active military duty.

Following work that Friday in October, Patrick was scheduled to head to Fairhope for a father-and-son hunting excursion—a ritual the two had shared since his childhood. But that morning, Patrick and two coworkers were sent into a huge circular silo to "walk down the corn": They were to loosen kernels around the walls so the corn would fall to the silo's middle, where it could be sucked to the floor by a huge fan. When one of the drifts collapsed, Patrick sank to his waist. His coworkers scrambled to help free him, but the fan pulled Patrick down until he was buried alive under an avalanche of corn. He had not been outfitted with a safety harness, which protects against this sort of accident.

Patrick was laid to rest the following Monday. Ron Hayes, who at the time oversaw the operations of a hospital outpatient center, spent that weekend in search of answers about the circumstances of his son's death. No one, however, could help.

Thus began a relentless search for the truth. Hayes called company officials and hounded an investigator in OSHA's Jacksonville, Florida office. He found a Mobile dock worker who had witnessed a similar tragedy a decade earlier and who could guide Hayes to experts in the field. Three weeks after his son's death, Hayes had already contacted grain facilities and industry organizations. He had spent hours in the library studying grain-handling and knew standard operating procedures. Within two months he had obtained a Dun & Bradstreet report on Showell Farms; he knew details of the company's inner workings and how many times it had been sued. He contacted the Florida state's attorney to ask—unsuccessfully—that Showell employees be deposed. He spoke with representatives of the De Funiak-area sheriff and fire departments for information about the tragedy. He called the state attorney general and met with a lawyer from that office. He even managed to get his hands on OSHA's field-operations manual—a blueprint for the agency's handling of such a case. Everyone Hayes turned to offered him help or information, and his investigative techniques seemed to be moving him toward the answers he so desperately sought.

Then, on February 4, 1994, some three months after the fatal accident, Hayes filed his first Freedom of Information Act request with OSHA. With that, everything changed.

The Freedom of Information Act (FOIA) was signed into law on Independence Day, 1966. The nation's media provided the lobbying impetus for passage of the legislation, which armed reporters with the means to ferret out important stories. At the same time, the law provided the average citizen better access to government information. Since then, countless FOIA requests have yielded documents on matters ranging from the mundane to the momentous. It has become a favored tool of muckrakers, although it is by and large still an under-utilized investigative device.

When Ron Hayes finally decided to make use of the law, he was warned that OSHA was notorious for sending out a few dozen-page samplers, rather than all the requested company information. Hayes indeed got such a pared-down compendium of documents, even though he'd learned that Showell Farms had been the subject of twen-

ty inspections over the previous eighteen years. So he took the pal-
try results of his FOIA inquiry to an OSHA official and insisted that
twenty inspections must have yielded far more data. "He said, 'You're
right,'" Hayes recalls. "And I said, 'There are thousands of documents,
and I want them all.'"

Hayes's request for *all* the documents wasn't mere hyperbole. He
believed that the evidence would demonstrate that his son's death
was willful—that the company knew the risks its employees were taking when they walked the corn. And as his inquiry continued, Hayes
came to believe that the culpability extended to OSHA, whose
regional office in Jacksonville was loath to prosecute companies for
willful death; instead, fines were levied against the offending companies. Then those fines were reduced or dropped altogether.

Hayes relentlessly pursued his search for documents, but there was
invariably a delay in receiving them. Such delays are hardly inconsequential, because OSHA cases are closed after six months and, barring
evidence of criminal intent, are never reopened. So an individual
hoping to prove that a family member's death was willful has little
time to unearth proof before the opportunity is gone forever.

As the months passed, additional roadblocks were put in Hayes's
path. In fact, he received some of the requested documents only after
a top OSHA official in Washington ordered the Jacksonville regional office to produce them.

One obstacle Hayes faced was that he didn't know what documents OSHA maintained and therefore didn't know what specifically
to ask for. This problem was solved, in part, by agency whistleblowers,
one of whom offered two explanations for helping Hayes: He wanted the frustrated investigator to know that there were indeed honest
agency employees, and the withholding of information piqued his
own curiosity. So the informant carefully reviewed the interoffice
memos and other materials that had been handed over by the
Jacksonville office, then instructed Hayes about what other documents he should request.

Hayes insisted that the director of OSHA's Jacksonville office had
bungled the investigation of his son's death, and an agency official
was dispatched to conduct an audit. The incident was deemed willful on the part of the company, and the auditor recommended a

$530,000 fine. But the Jacksonville official ruled that the willful claim was not supported by the evidence and reduced the fine to $30,000. A confidential case file detailing this series of events was subsequently sent to Washington—its existence made known to Hayes by one of his confidential informants. His FOIA request for the file went unheeded, so five months later he asked one of his U.S. Senators to intercede. By week's end, Hayes had those files, too.

Sometimes he was forced to go to ridiculous lengths to track down documents. For example, a year after his son's death, Hayes learned through an informant that employees in one OSHA office had been instructed not to release documents to him. This informant gave Hayes a file citation, and Hayes in turn had a friend file a FOIA request under his dog's name. "They answered that boy's dog on the same day," says an exasperated Hayes. "They gave the dog more information than they gave me." The technique proved so effective that Hayes later filed a FOIA under an acquaintance's name. The result: OSHA responded in a day with a 423-page file.

It's no wonder, then, that Hayes has mixed emotions about the Freedom of Information Act. "I call it the Fighting for Information Act," he says. "There's nothing free about it. The time and money expended to get a few documents is unbelievable."

But these battles for documents never deterred Hayes, who repeatedly filed appeals when his requests were denied. A denied appeal may be challenged in court, and Hayes availed himself of the opportunity to do so. While an attorney can be helpful in such matters, Hayes pursued the legal action on his own. He spent days in a law library reading about FOIA and scrutinizing previous suits. Then he wrote his own suit and paid the $152 fee to file it in U.S. District Court. The night before his first court appearance, he studied legal terms so he'd understand the judge's questions.

Hayes's fight attracted the attention of *Dateline NBC* and a number of newspapers. His methodical search for documents and his ability to back up claims with evidence gave him credibility with reporters. Because he had also documented every conversation in a diary—a technique he recommends to others—he could further substantiate his claims of wrongdoing within Showell Farms and OSHA.

Hayes earned such respect, in fact, that he was called upon to testify before a U.S. Senate committee investigating OSHA. Following the appearance, Hayes and his wife met with then-Labor Secretary Robert Reich and other top Labor Department officials. The couple was given a letter from the director of OSHA apologizing for the way their son's death was investigated. As a result of Hayes's actions, the letter added, the agency had reworked its standards for the protection of grain-handling workers.

Such a victory may have sent others on to new pursuits, but not Hayes. He founded an organization called the FIGHT (Families in Grief Hold Together) Project to help the families of workers killed in workplace accidents, and he resigned his hospital job to devote himself to it full-time.

Hayes helps these survivors wage their own battle with OSHA. This assistance naturally includes schooling them in the art of FOIA: When someone contacts FIGHT, Hayes sends out a packet with an extremely broad, model FOIA letter. "I felt like if I asked for everything but their underwear, they'd have to respond," he says.

And if there is no response, Hayes is prepared to intervene on their behalf. "I'll call the D.C. office in a heartbeat and chew them out, and it ain't but a couple of days before I get the information," he says.

Freedom Trail

There's no shortage of good information on using the federal Freedom of Information Act to your advantage. Here are three of the best, most comprehensive resources:

A Citizen's Guide on Using the Freedom of Information Act and the Privacy Act of 1974 to Request Government Records: First Report by the House Committee on Government Operations
Subcommittee on Information, Justice, Transportation, and Agriculture, 1993 edition
House Report 103-104, 103rd Congress, 1st Session

The guide is available in many libraries and may be purchased from Government Printing Office bookstores. It's also available at no cost on the Internet. The address is: **www.cpsr.org/cpsr/foia /citizens_guide_to_foia_93.txt**.

The Freedom of Information Act: A User's Guide
By the Freedom of Information Clearinghouse

The clearinghouse is a nonprofit project of Ralph Nader's Center for Study of Responsive Law. It provides technical and legal assistance to individuals, public-interest groups, and the media. Contact the clearinghouse at: P.O. Box 19367, Washington, D.C. 20036; (202) 588-7790. The guide can be downloaded for free from the clearing-house's Web site: www.citizen.org/litigation/foic/foilguid.html.

The Web site of the Society of Professional Journalists includes an array of valuable FOIA resources, including links to federal-agency FOIA contacts and capsule summaries of state FOIA laws. The address is: www.spj.org/foia/index.htm.

Twelve Steps to FOIA Success

1. The Freedom of Information Act only entitles citizens to existing records, which means that agencies are not obligated to collect or analyze information for you. So when preparing a request, always try to hone in on specific documents.

2. Address your request to the proper agency—that is, the one with responsibility for the program of interest to you. Two good sources for identifying the right agency are the Federal Information Center, (fic.info.gov or by telephone 800-688-9889) a program overseen by the U.S. General Services Administration, and the *United States Government Manual*, (www.access.gpo.gov /nara/nara001.html, also available in printed form from the Government Printing Office) which includes addresses for agency headquarters and field offices.

3. Call the agency and speak to someone about the documents you're seeking. You may be provided with information that will help

narrow your request. What's more, if that agency doesn't maintain the records you're seeking, the staff may be able to identify the proper agency.

4. Your FOIA letter should be addressed to the agency's FOIA officer. Write "Freedom of Information Act Request" on the envelope.

5. Include your name, address, and phone number on the FOIA letter. If an agency FOIA officer has questions about your request, a phone call can speed up the process.

6. The letter should be brief and simple. It should indicate that the request is being made under the Freedom of Information Act.

7. By law, the letter must "reasonably describe" the records you want. That means you must provide enough detail to permit agency staff to locate the records. So be as precise as possible, including names, dates, and addresses whenever possible.

8. If you can't identify specific records, clearly explain what you're looking for.

9. The law mandates that fees must be waived or reduced if disclosure of the information is in the public interest. Therefore, include in your letter a request for a waiver or a reduction of fees. In addition, ask to be notified in advance if search and copying fees will exceed a fixed amount. When appropriate, explain how disclosure of the requested records will contribute to public understanding of the operations or activities of the government.

10. If you want computer records or records in a form other than paper, state this clearly in your request.

11. Follow up your request with a phone call.

12. Keep a copy of the request letter along with copies of any additional correspondence. Also keep records of phone conversations.

You Can't Always Get What You Want

Filing a FOIA request does not guarantee that you'll end up with the documents you're seeking. There are, in fact, nine specific exemptions that can turn your quest for information into a futile exercise:

1. **Classified documents.** Agencies may withhold documents classified in the interest of national defense or foreign policy. The rules for classification are established by the President and not by FOIA or other laws. Classified documents may, however, be requested under FOIA. An agency can then review the requested documents to determine if they still require protection.

2. **Internal personnel rules and practices.** This primarily includes documents, handbooks, and the like related to internal agency procedures.

3. **Information exempted by another federal statute.** This exemption applies only if the other statute clearly and unequivocally requires that the documents be withheld from the public.

4. **Confidential business information.** This generally covers trade secrets—a recipe for a commercial food product, for example—and privileged commercial or financial information obtained from an individual or company. This would include information on a company's marketing plans, profits, or costs that, if disclosed, would likely harm its competitive position. Information created by an agency on its own cannot normally be withheld under this exemption.

5. **Internal government communications.** This includes such documents as correspondence between government departments about pending decisions or internal memoranda describing options for conducting an agency's business.

6. **Documents related to personal privacy.** This includes personnel, medical, and similar files that, if made public, would constitute a clearly unwarranted invasion of personal privacy.

7. **Investigatory records.** Covered under this exemption are law-enforcement records that might identify confidential sources, endanger someone's life, divulge police techniques, or interfere with ongoing proceedings.

8. **Financial institution records.** This protects information prepared by or for the Federal Deposit Insurance Corporation, the Federal Reserve, and other agencies that regulate financial institutions.

9. **Geological information.** This rarely used exemption covers geological and geophysical information about oil wells.

State of the States

Every state has its own corollary to the federal Freedom of Information Act, but as would-be document hunters can testify, not all of these laws are as user-friendly as FOIA. While the agencies and departments of some states willingly and expeditiously process open-records requests, the personnel in other states sometimes act as if they're either above the law or entirely unfamiliar with it. In fact, while state FOIA laws typically forbid agency staff from asking questions about why documents are being requested or the affiliation of the individual seeking them, those processing the requests sometimes do so anyway. In some instances, they may intimate—or even state outright—that requests not meeting their personal criteria will be denied.

To complicate matters, state and local agencies may have wide latitude in assessing fees, the law mandating only, for example, that they charge citizens a "reasonable" amount. As a result, documents handed over gratis in one jurisdiction may cost a dollar per page in another, while agencies within a state may also have dramatically different fee schedules. Local-government fees may be all over the map as well, with citizens apparently at the mercy of the keeper of the documents. For example, when three Chicago-area students investigated local jurisdictions' FOIA practices, they found fees ranging from a nickel per page to two dollars. Never mind that Illinois law prohibits public bodies from charging copying fees that exceed the actual reproduction costs. As a result, it's a good idea to check the state's FOIA laws before filing a request. You may learn, for instance, that the law allows citizens to bring their own equipment to copy documents—a potential money saver for those with access to a portable copying machine or optical scanner.

Also consider the advice of Chicago attorney Richard Means, a FOIA expert who has used the law to unearth intriguing documents for public scrutiny. (See Chapter Nine for the full story of Means's Public Access Project.) Means has exploited a little-known provision in the Illinois Freedom of Information Act (also found in the federal law) that requires every public agency to prepare and maintain "a reasonably current list of all types and categories of records under its control." Such a list, says Means, can be valuable in several ways, including:

- The list may identify documents by their proper names, removing a potential barrier to disclosure. For example, a request for an agency "budget" may be refused as unavailable if the agency calls the document its "appropriation ordinance."

- The easy availability of various agency lists can narrow a document search to a particular governmental body. This can speed retrieval by obviating the need to ask several agencies and wait weeks for replies.

- The absence of a particular record or category of records from an agency list may be reasonably interpreted as either a denial of that record's availability or an indication that the agency seeks to hide the information. That should help guide a researcher's method of attempting to obtain access to the records.

Means has requested such lists of available documents from state, county, and city offices. It's a project that has proved meaningful in Illinois, and one that can be easily emulated in states with similar disclosure provisions.

In Denial

The denial of a FOIA request is not necessarily the end of the story. There is a formal appeals process that can turn a rejection into a sheaf of documents, and it generally involves nothing more than writing another letter.

Here are a half-dozen tips for winning round two:

- An agency must inform you of its reasons for denial. If your request was denied because it was too broad or vague, revise your original letter and file it again. In addition, consider filing a similar request with other agencies that may keep duplicate or similar records.

- You may appeal a request that was even partially denied. So if you think the withholding of some documents was unwarranted, you may appeal that decision without jeopardizing the release of other materials. Similarly, you have the right to appeal the imposition of fees that you believe are too high or unwarranted.

- Your appeal should be addressed to the head of the agency. "Freedom of Information Act Appeal" should be written on the envelope. The appeal letter should include a description and a copy of your request, plus an explanation of why you believe your request should have been honored. Bear in mind that an agency may release records at its discretion, even if those documents are covered by one of the nine exemptions. There are no fees associated with a letter of appeal.

- Don't wait too long to file an appeal. There's always the risk that documents may be destroyed in the meantime, so waiting could preclude hope of getting necessary papers.

- If your appeal is denied, try seeking help from your Members of Congress, who may be able to intervene on your behalf. Also consult the Freedom of Information Clearinghouse (see page 19) or other FOIA experts for ideas on how to refile your request.

- When all else fails, you may take a FOIA case to court. Suits may be filed in the U.S. District Court, either where you live or in the District of Columbia. It's possible to initiate such litigation without an attorney, but a competent FOIA lawyer is likely to give you a substantial edge. And even if you ultimately lose the case, the agency may release some of the documents during the proceedings. If you win, the agency will be ordered to turn over all the requested documents.

SAMPLE FOIA REQUEST LETTER

Date

Agency Head [or Freedom of Information Act Officer]
Name of Agency
Address of Agency
City, State, Zip code

Dear   :

This is a request under the Freedom of Information Act.

I request that a copy of the following documents [or documents containing the following information] be provided to me: [Identify the documents as specifically as possible].

In order to help determine my status to assess fees, you should know that I am an individual seeking information for personal rather than commercial use.

[Optional] I request a waiver of all fees for this request as permitted under the act. Disclosure of the requested information to me is in the public interest because it is likely to contribute significantly to public understanding of the operations or activities of the government. However, if there are any search or copying fees, please inform me before you fill the request.

Thank you for your consideration.

Sincerely,

Name
Address
City, State, Zip Code
Phone number [optional]

SAMPLE FOIA APPEAL LETTER

Date

Agency Head [or Freedom of Information Act Appeal Officer]
Name of Agency
Address of Agency
City, State, Zip Code

Dear   :

This is an appeal under the Freedom of Information Act.

On [date], I requested documents under the Freedom of Information Act. My request was assigned the following identification number: _____. On [date], I received a response to my request in a letter signed by [name of official]. I appeal the denial of my request for access to [description of the documents].

[Optional] I appeal the decision to deny my request for a waiver of fees. I believe that I am entitled to a waiver of fees. Disclosure of the documents I requested is in the public interest because the information is likely to contribute significantly to public understanding of the operations or activities of the government and is not primarily in my commercial interest.

[Optional] I appeal the decision to require me to pay review costs for this request. I am not seeking the documents for a commercial use. [Provide details.]

Thank you for your consideration of this appeal.

Sincerely,

Name
Address
City, State, Zip Code
Phone number [optional]

CHAPTER TWO

Making a Federal Case of It

Exposing a suspect federal-government program may be a noble deed, but the whistleblowers often face the same perplexing question: Is anyone out there listening?

When Ed Block is asked to trace the unlikely demise of his professional life, he pauses briefly before singling out a February morning in 1983 as the moment it began unraveling. Block remembers those events well: He cruised into a service station and phoned his Philadelphia office to say that his Triumph Spitfire had developed brake problems and that he'd be on his way after a brief delay. But an hour later, Block called again to say that the repairs would be more complicated than anticipated and he'd have to miss a day's work.

Block never thought this unexpected absence would have any job-related consequences. After all, in the nine years he had labored for the federal Defense Logistics Agency, he had proved himself to be an uncommonly valuable employee. The four-year Navy veteran, whose service record included a specialty in antisubmarine warfare, had carved out a unique niche for himself as the military's senior equipment specialist in wire and cable. Block served as liaison between Defense and private-sector suppliers, seeing to it that the government spent its money on products made to specification. He was enthusiastic about his work and, by all accounts, good at it: In 1981, for example, his multibillion-dollar cost-saving efforts earned him an Employee of the Year award from among his 2,000 coworkers.

But two years later, as the Reagan-era military buildup was going into overdrive, doing good actually proved to be Block's undoing. After blowing the whistle on what he says were deliberate purchases of unsafe wiring—components that would jeopardize the safety of those flying military aircraft—he found himself in the Defense Department's crosshairs. "I was thinking, if the higher-ups find out about this they'll say, 'Thanks for saving the day,'" he says. "Instead, I was greeted with bare teeth."

For reasons Block did not yet fully understand, those higher-ups wanted the wiring contract to proceed as planned. And they wanted their underling to drop his objections and get with the program. But by his own admission, Block was naïve about the potential consequences of pursuing the truth. "I had no idea what was going on," he says. "I thought the good guy always wins."

He adds: "They unleashed the dragon on me."

Indeed, Block got his first inkling of the battle's fierceness the day after his auto mishap—an event he had written off as mere nuisance. But after arriving at work, he was charged with being AWOL.

"I still didn't know what they were doing," he recalls, stunned at the developments.

He would soon find out.

Ed Block is a patriot, and proud of it. His second cousin helped raise the American flag on Iwo Jima, his father was a career Navy man, and Block traces his lineage to *The Mayflower*. "I'm not a commie," he says, edgy about the heat he's taken over weighing in against the Pentagon. "I'm not Chicken Little. I'm a regular guy who excelled in the job. I became the tops in my field."

He also became entangled in an increasingly nightmarish controversy that shook the foundation of his belief system. All he sought to do, he says, was inform his superiors that he'd discovered problems with Poly-X, a type of wiring manufactured by California-based Raychem Corporation. Block claimed that the wiring was both inferior and overpriced, and that its use in F-14 fighters was implicated in a series of unexplained crashes. He also insisted that Raychem was using underhanded tactics to secure lucrative sole-source contracts, and that those high up in the command needed to address such shortcomings of the procurement process.

But Block was hardly encouraged to pursue his suspicions. Instead, he says, he was urged to squelch his criticism of this contractor's wiring and just do his job. "I was told point-blank that if you don't drop this, the full force of the government will be brought against you. I thought, How could I be significant enough to have the whole Department of Defense come after me?"

Here's how: High-ranking members of the military, Block would later allege, were offered deals by the wire maker to protect its financial interest. As a result, he adds, when he failed to shelve his complaints, his career was systematically dismantled. He was reassigned. And finally, in 1984, he was charged with falsifying $43 on an expense-account report—a crime he insists was fabricated, but one that was nonetheless punished by the termination of his government service.

Block had become the self-described "poster boy of Retaliation 101."

Now what?

Ed Block asked himself that repeatedly after seeing his livelihood taken away. He was offered an industry consulting job but feared that taking part in the revolving-door system that he knew was an ingredient of the Poly-X fiasco would tarnish his reputation. On the other hand, he believed, collecting unemployment would make it appear as if he'd accepted the military's decision and agreed with it. So instead, Block worked a series of menial jobs while pondering his future. The economic consequences were devastating for him and his family, but he still couldn't walk away from the fight. "I was the wide-eyed optimist," he says. "I thought, What am I left with if I put it down? It's either going to kill me or I'm going to win."

For Block, winning wasn't about financial remuneration but rather about winning back his job, having his reputation restored, and letting an uninformed public know about a potentially disastrous situation. After all, not only did Raychem supply the military with wire and cable, but the commercial airline industry used the same components.

The problem, says Block, is that the protective coating around Poly-X is prone to cracking with age, thereby exposing the wire's metal and in turn causing electrical arcing. If an aircraft's fuel tanks are nearby, the resulting sparks can ignite an explosion and cause a midair fire. In meetings with the Center, Raychem has adamantly denied Block's charges.

The Navy finally stopped using the wiring, but the commercial carriers, Block contends, weren't told of the problem. As a result, the suspect wiring was installed in such aircraft as the Boeing 747, including the one carrying passengers on the ill-fated TWA Flight 800, which crashed into the Atlantic Ocean in July 1996.

It was the potential for that sort of disaster that kept Block on a mission to expose the problems with Poly-X. He filed more than a hundred Freedom of Information Act requests for documents that would help support his contention. He amassed a stack of records. He contacted Members of Congress and shared his findings with committee investigators. He developed a wide array of sources in every corner of the aviation industry, including mechanics, air-traffic controllers, and whistleblowers at such companies as McDonnell-Douglas. He shared his findings with groups whose family members had perished in airline accidents. He studied the wire installed in ValuJet Flight 592, which went down in the Florida Everglades in 1996. He badgered the Federal Aviation Administration and the National Transportation Safety Board (NTSB) to consider his findings. He called print reporters and TV newsmagazine producers.

But for all his efforts, Block's decade-long campaign was largely ignored. "There are days you feel drained," he admits. "You feel, I've tried everything and cried the voice in the wilderness."

It was, then, something of a vindication for Block when his U.S. Representative convened a closed-door session in April 1997 to explore Block's theories. On hand that day were representatives of the FBI, the General Accounting Office, the Navy, and other federal agencies. After futile searches for answers to the causes of the TWA and ValuJet disasters, Block's ideas were suddenly gaining some credence. In fact, the FAA soon ordered that 747 wiring be inspected because of the possibility that abrasion could result in electrical arcing and cause fire or fuel-tank explosion.

According to Block, the NTSB's own databases include more than two dozen incidents involving electrical-wiring malfunction from 1983 to 1995. He adds that Navy officials admitted during the meeting that hundreds of F-14s were grounded in the mid-1980s because the cost of replacing the wiring wasn't feasible.

Following the Capitol Hill session, Block got a chance to air his faulty-wire theory on the ABC newsmagazine *Prime Time Live*. Other media appearances followed, as increasing attention was paid to his allegations.

Block doesn't know if he'll ever be entirely vindicated, but he has no plans to give up the fight. In addition to his search for additional data, he counsels other whistleblowers who he thinks are unfairly vilified. Ironically, federal agencies still seek his expertise. He serves on an FAA advisory committee and was also consulted about the February 1998 accident in which a Marine jet clipped a ski-lift cable in Italy, killing twenty.

Ultimately, though, what Block really wants is what he wanted all along: "To me the only thing I'd like to see happen is that they face the facts and I have my name cleared. I come from a long line of American bluebloods. I take my name seriously and don't want to be thought of as a rabble-rouser."

Block would also like his job back. He still has a great interest in wire and cable. He still has a commitment to his cause. And he still remembers the unraveling of his life as if it were yesterday, not a decade and a half ago.

In fact, Block still recalls the details of the fateful day that his Triumph Spitfire broke down. The car, it turned out, had problems with the electrical wiring—a detail not lost on the good-natured Block.

But he's not surprised. It turns out he owned another car that had been brought to the repair shop forty times. "They put on the most elaborate test equipment," he says. "Finally, the mechanic called and said the problem was bare wires under the wheel well that were touching each other and shorting out.

"It shows you how underappreciated wiring is."

Unearthing Government Documents

It's not always necessary to file a Freedom of Information Act request to come up with valuable documents. The U.S. government is a publisher without peer, and the data you need may be readily available in government studies, reports, databases, newsletters, bulletins, circulars, manuals, handbooks, press releases, and so on. All you have to do is track down citations, then get your hands on the actual materials.

That, however, is sometimes easier said than done. The huge volume of titles can be overwhelming, turning a seemingly routine search into a frustrating—and ultimately futile—exercise.

But there are methodical ways to approach the hunt for government information. Moreover, you don't need to be in Washington, D.C., to put your hands on what you need.

Indexes and Finding Aids

The federal government makes available a variety of indexes and finding aids that will help in the search for publications of possible interest. Many are available in public libraries, either in a printed format or on CD-ROM. Some are also accessible via the Internet.

- The *Monthly Catalog of United States Government Publications* (MOCAT), issued by the Superintendent of Documents, is the most comprehensive compilation of available government publications. The catalog includes most of the information made available through the Federal Depository Library Program (see below), and because it's indexed by author, title, subject, series/report number, contract number, and stock number, finding pertinent materials is not difficult. MOCAT can also be searched online on the GPO Access Web site. Simply enter one or more search terms, and the search engine returns as many as one thousand citations along with the Superintendent of Documents catalog number. Many documents may then be viewed online, while others can be ordered from the GPO. The Web site address is **www.access.gpo.gov/su_docs/dpos/adpos400.html**.

- Publications Reference File is a guide that lists all government information products offered for sale by the Superintendent of Documents. PRF is available in a bimonthly microfiche edition found in many libraries. It's also searchable online under the title Sales Product Catalog at no cost. The address is **https:// orders.access.gpo.gov/su_docs/sale/prf/prf.html**.

- Marcive GPO CAT/PAC Plus is one of the commercially pro-duced guides to government information. This CD-ROM index, available in many libraries, is easy to use and has some advantages over the GPO's Internet-based system. For example, Marcive cat-alogs documents from 1976 to present, while GPO includes only a few years. Marcive's menu-driven software also lets users limit searches by years. The Marcive database is also searchable on the Internet for a fee. The address is www.marcive.com/Web1.htm.

- FirstSearch is another set of commercially produced databases available for searching in many libraries. The GPO Database includes citations to more than a half-million items covering all subject areas of interest to the U.S. government. Searches can be limited by year, serials, maps, videos, computer files, and so on.

Locating the Documents

Documents available online, such as many of those listed on MOCAT's Web site, are of course just a mouse click away. But get-ting copies of other documents requires a little more work.

When you find a citation to a government information product, record the "SuDoc" (short for Superintendent of Documents) number. This document identifier begins with a capital letter (an agency iden-tifier) and is followed by a string of numbers. The materials may then be ordered from one of the 24 GPO bookstores around the country, from the GPO Order Desk at (202) 512-1800, or from the GPO Online Bookstore at **www.access.gpo.gov/su_docs/sale.html**.

You may also examine them at a federal depository library. There are about 1,350 such libraries throughout the U.S., at least one in almost every congressional district. Be forewarned that depository libraries do not typically receive every government publication, so call ahead first. But all provide free public access to a wide variety of government information in both print and electronic formats, and many permit users to borrow the materials.

- Call your U.S. Representative to find the location of the federal depository library in your area. A state- and area-code-searchable database of depository libraries can be found at **www.access.gpo.gov/su_docs/dpos/adpos003.html**.

Government Gumshoes

The General Accounting Office is the investigative arm of Congress. It examines matters related to the receipt and disbursement of public funds, evaluating government programs and activities at the request of federal legislators.

GAO reports can be valuable tools for anyone engaged in research, and therefore should be on every muckraker's list of potential resources. Many public libraries receive notices of new GAO reports, single copies of which are available at no cost at the agency's Washington headquarters or by writing: U.S. General Accounting Office, P.O. Box 37050, Washington, D.C. 20013. Phone orders may be placed by calling (202) 512-6000. You can also place orders on GAO's Web site at www.gao.gov.

But perhaps more valuable than the reports themselves is the manual that these government sleuths rely on to help plan their searches. The *Investigators' Guide to Sources of Information*, first published in 1995, is a trove of information sources. The *Guide* will help you navigate the mazes of federal, state, and local agencies. The 113-page manual will tip you off to a wide variety of documents that you might not otherwise have known existed. For example, you know that the tax collector happily takes your money, but you may not have realized that a tax-collector office maintains the following information:

- names and addresses of payers of property taxes, including payers who are not the apparent owners
- legal descriptions of property
- amounts of taxes paid on real and personal property

- delinquency status of taxes
- names of former owners of property

In addition, the guide devotes considerable space to electronic databases and finding information on the Internet. It's by far one of the more valuable reference works, and it (along with recent GAO reports) can be downloaded at no cost from the GAO's Web site at: www.gao.gov.

Is There a Docket in the House?

An out-of-town company has received a contract to build a municipal building, and a laborer tips you off that the firm appears to be cutting corners—a practice that might one day jeopardize the safety of those who work there. You begin an investigation of the construction company and learn that one of the partners owned another business that was involved in some sort of messy lawsuit. Naturally, you want details, and you also want to determine whether this person has been involved in other legal actions that might be pertinent.

The local courthouse is one place to look. (For details, see Chapter Four.) A law library may also provide answers, but it is invariably a confusing place for a novice researcher. The card catalog is of no help, and finding cases appears at first to be a needle-in-a-haystack exercise.

But researching cases is really not difficult. It basically involves finding citations and then deciphering them.

Finding Cases

Your goal is to find case citations, and that's done by using one or more of the digests that you'll find in a law library. There are digests that cover cases brought in one particular state. There are also regional digests (the South Eastern Digest includes cases from Georgia, the Carolinas, Virginia, and West Virginia), federal court digests, and so on.

The digest system indexes only "reported" cases—that is, ones of legal importance. (A company suing a homeowner over nonpayment of a bill, for example, would not be reported; neither would uncontested matters, nor cases that are quickly settled or plea-bargained.) Each digest has a Table of Cases arranged alphabetically by the names of the parties to the lawsuit. Recent cases are published in stand-alone paper supplements or smaller supplements that are fitted into pockets in the back of the hardback volumes.

If you know the case name and the court that decided it, go directly to the appropriate digest and search the alphabetical listings in the Table of Cases. If you know when the case was decided but not the court, search the Table of Cases in a Decennial Digest. Each of these volumes covers a particular time period. (The *Tenth Decennial Digest*, for example, includes cases reported from 1986 to 1991.) If you don't know when the case was decided, start with the Tenth Decennial Digest and work backward to the Ninth, Eighth, and so on. Keep in mind that only a fraction of all cases are reported in these digests. For instance, decisions from state trial courts are rarely reported; instead, copies of decisions and other documents from these cases must be obtained from the clerk of that particular court. And, because digests and case reporters are designed for research on what the law is, even a reported decision may mention only a few of the facts of the case.

Deciphering Citations

When you do find a case of interest, the digest will give you a citation. This is a roadmap to tracking down the actual decision. A case citation consists of the following:

- The parties to the lawsuit listed by surnames, plaintiff followed by defendant.
- The volume number of the case reporter that contains the text of the decision.
- The abbreviated name of the case reporter.
- The page on which the case begins.
- The abbreviated name of the court that issued the decision, listed in parentheses.
- The year the case was decided, also inside the parentheses.

- There may also be supplemental information, such as a listing for another reporter in which the case can be found.

For example, here's how to dissect *Mulcahey v. Columbia Organic Chemicals Company, Inc.*, 29 F.3d 148 (4th Cir. 1994):

- The name of the case is *Mulcahey v. Columbia Organic Chemicals Company, Inc.*

- The case can be found in the 29th volume of the Federal Reporter, third series.

- The case begins on page 148.

- It was decided in the United States Court of Appeals for the Fourth Circuit in 1994.

The only remaining task is to find the Federal Reporter, third series, in the stacks. A dictionary of legal abbreviations, available in the library's reference section, will help you decipher the citations. Here are standard abbreviations for the most widely used federal and regional reporters:

A., A.2d – Atlantic Reporter, Atlantic Reporter second series

Cal. Rptr., Cal. Rptr. 2d – California Reporter, California Reporter second series

F., F.2d, F.3d – Federal Reporter, Federal Reporter second series, and third series

F. Supp. – Federal Supplement

N.E., N.E.2d – North Eastern Reporter, North Eastern Reporter second series

N.W., N.W.2d – North Western Reporter, North Western Reporter second series

N.Y.S., N.Y.S.2d – New York Supplement, New York Supplement second series

P., P.2d – Pacific Reporter, Pacific Reporter second series

S. Ct. – Supreme Court Reporter

S.E., S.E.2d – South Eastern Reporter, South Eastern Reporter second series

So., So.2d – Southern Reporter, Southern Reporter second series
S.W., S.W.2d – South Western Reporter, South Western Reporter
  second series
U.S. – United States Reports

(The United States Reports is an "official" reporter, published by the federal government. The others listed are all produced by West Publishing.)

CAR Trips

There are long rows of shelves in the Library of Congress filled with hundreds of residential phone books. If you're looking for the phone number of someone of unknown address, you can spend a day poring through these paper volumes. With any luck, you may turn up the number long before your alphabetical search through the states brings you to Wisconsin or Wyoming.

On the other hand, you can simply try a no-cost Internet-accessible search mechanism like Switchboard (www.switchboard.com), AnyWho (www.anywho.com), Infospace.com (www.infospace.com), or Lycos' WhoWhere (www.whowhere.lycos.com/Phone). Type in the person's name, hit "Search," count to two (four or five if you have a slow modem), and if the number is listed, you'll probably have it.

If you have a phone number but no name to go with it, and no access to a crisscross directory for that city, you can spend another day in the Library of Congress searching through every listing in the book. Or you can type the number into the reverse-search function of 411.com (www.411.com) or infoUSA (www.infousa.com). In moments, you'll have the name and address.

But what if the person you're in search of is a student? Get back on the World Wide Web and try this address: www.uiuc.edu/cgibin /ph/lookup?Query=. (for the most direct route, include the final period in the URL). From there you'll be able to search the campus phone books of hundreds of colleges.

Computer-assisted reporting (CAR) is a powerful tool that enhances your odds of digging up information. The technology offers fast and easy access to commercial and governmental information alike, either via online databases or CD-ROMs and other media. In either case, CAR gives you a decided edge.

There are numerous CAR strategies, depending on what sort of information you're after. One of the best manuals for learning these techniques is available from Investigative Reporters and Editors (see page 106 for more information about IRE, including address and ordering information for publications):

- *Computer-Assisted Reporting: A Practical Guide.* This comprehensive guide to the high-tech techniques of investigative reporting was authored by Brant Houston, executive director of Investigative Reporters and Editors. The book offers step-by-step procedures for using databases, the Internet, and other online resources. Included is a diskette containing exercises to help you hone your skills. Cost: $30.

Appropriately enough, there are also some excellent CAR primers and other resources available on the Internet. These include:

- The National Institute for Computer-Assisted Reporting is a program of the Investigative Reporters and Editors and the University of Missouri School of Journalism, where it is based. NICAR trains journalists in the use of databases, and it is a great repository of information on the subject. Among the things you'll find on NICAR's Web site is a "net tour," offering dozens of links to useful sources, databases, and search engines. Several reporters also provide their personal lists of favorite Internet resources. It's all available at www.nicar.org.

- FACSNET ACSNET is a service for journalists provided by the Foundation for American Communications (FACS) in partnership with the San Diego Supercomputer Center. A number of major news organizations helped launch the Web site, which includes a variety of Internet resources and reporting tools. In the CARS section, for example, there are tips on how to effectively use vehicle registration information and marriage and divorce records. The address is www.facsnet.org/cgi-bin/main.cgi.

Muckraking 101
Lesson One: What's Going On?

Imagine that you're a member of the citizens' advisory board that monitors the activities of your hometown zoo. In your role, you have regular dealings with both the zoo director and Animal Pals, the non-profit organization whose fundraising activities help supplement the zoo's municipal budget. Everyone is cordial, because everyone is working for the same goals: to ensure that the animals are well treated and that zoo-goers have a positive experience.

Now imagine that a disgruntled keeper at the Ebbinger Zoo tips you off to something unusual: For the past few years, a man with no apparent zoo affiliation has hauled away dozens of animals. Questions about the man's identity have been deflected by the zoo's director, piquing the small staff's curiosity. Your tipster fears that something isn't kosher and urges you to investigate.

The next day you call an old buddy at an out-of-town zoo to ask his opinion. He says that it sounds like a curious arrangement, and he puts you in touch with a colleague at another zoo, who concurs. So at the next advisory-board meeting you confront the director. He claims that such matters are beyond the board's purview, but when you press him for an answer he insists that this is much ado about nothing. The man in question, who hails from a town in the southern part of the state, is not only a reputable animal dealer, but he's also involved with breeding programs designed to ensure the survival of endangered species. What's more, says the director, the dealer bought only two or three animals, and the fees he paid were used to upgrade the facilities for the zoo's collection. End of story.

The other board members aren't sure what to make of all this but agree to move on to other business when the town's mayor says that he's both satisfied with the explanation and, truth be told, indebted to the zoo director for years of good work. But your instincts tell you there's indeed more to the story, that this arrangement doesn't seem quite right. When the meeting adjourns, you vow to get to the bottom of it.

Now what?

If muckraking had hard-and-fast rules, your task would be a cinch: contact this regulatory agency or that, dig out invoices and contracts, copy some records, file a FOIA, search a few databases, assemble some newspaper clippings, and your answer would materialize like a Polaroid picture taken a minute earlier.

But investigative reporting is, unfortunately, a lot more complex. There is no simple formula, no precise roadmap that will always take you from the start of an investigation to its finish. Instead, this kind of reporting typically requires a practitioner to learn the fundamentals and then improvise—to backtrack from the blind alleys and try another course of action. Sometimes the answers are behind the next door; other times they're at the end of a seemingly endless maze. And as even the most seasoned veteran will tell you, occasionally there is nothing but a dead end down a one-way street.

In this case, however, there are certainly numerous avenues to pursue. After all, the zoo is municipally funded, federally inspected, and subject to state regulations. The zoo director let out the man's name and hometown. And you've got to figure that any animal dealer breeding endangered species must need some sort of permit. If there's something illegal or unsavory going on, there must be a way to find that out.

Indeed, there may be. Follow along on a six-part quest to learn whether the tipster's concerns—and the board member's suspicions— were in fact well founded. It's a hypothetical exercise, but the techniques used and sources consulted—all highlighted in **boldface**— will give you insight into the elaborate, multifaceted game plan that a savvy muckraker might devise. Of course, this novice already has at least part of the routine figured out: The first step was to **ask experts** in the field for background information. The next step, on page 60, involves the search for threads to follow.

Next: Getting Up to Speed

CHAPTER THREE

State Secrets

*The letters that flood Jim McCloskey's offices are from inmates
who know they'll remain guilty until proven innocent. They also
know that McCloskey may be their only hope.*

As usual, Jim McCloskey is waiting. This time he's waiting for a
late-August court hearing that he's certain will free Eddie
Baker from the Pennsylvania prison cell that Baker has
wrongly occupied for the last 23 years. Baker first contacted
McCloskey a decade earlier, insisting in a letter that he was innocent
of the murder charges brought against him when he was just seventeen years old. Baker wanted McCloskey's assistance. There was
nowhere else to turn.

Eddie Baker thought his handwritten appeal might somehow bring
a swift reversal of a misguided verdict; instead he found himself at the
end of a perpetually long line: McCloskey's nonprofit organization,
Centurion Ministries, receives a thousand or so pleas each year from
those claiming to have been unfairly sentenced to death or to long-
term incarceration. All want McCloskey to help overturn their
convictions. All want the investigative muscle of Centurion's small
staff, which over the course of a decade and a half has managed to
rescue both lifers and death-row inmates from seemingly irreversible
fates.

Because all petitioners receive at least some consideration,
Centurion's assistance is inevitably a long time coming. In fact, seven
years passed before McCloskey finally told Baker he was convinced
of the convict's innocence and would therefore take on his case. That
news may have resuscitated Baker's hopes of winning a speedy release,

but he soon learned otherwise: Once Centurion agrees to act on someone's behalf, those eventually granted their freedom typically must
wait three to six years for release from prison. Like McCloskey, who
over the years has learned the virtues of patience, Eddie Baker could
only wait.

But now, in the summer of 1997, the wait appeared to be almost
over. In one week, a Philadelphia judge would rule on whether recently revealed evidence demanded that Baker be granted a new trial.
McCloskey was confident that Baker would be the nineteenth inmate
he'd helped free. After all, McCloskey had doggedly pursued the truth
in this matter, scouring Baker's South Philadelphia neighborhood for
witnesses who could identify the real murderer.

It was not an easy search. It never is.

Sometimes McCloskey simply knocks on doors and explains himself—a tactic that often results in his being mistakenly branded a
police officer or an FBI agent. Whenever possible, however, he tries to
elicit help from the community with a soft-sell approach that relies
on introductions. "You have to have a nice personality," he says. "You
can't be intimidating. We have to have people like us, feel comfortable with us, and trust us.

"It's easy if you have someone working with you who's influential
in that person's life," he adds. "We'll go to a witness and persuade him
to meet with us. The witness knows he has the blessing of people close
to him."

The Eddie Baker investigation brought McCloskey straight to the
inmate's family. They sent McCloskey to neighbors, who in turn
referred him to others in the community. Finally, the trial led him to a
onetime convict familiar with McCloskey's success in springing
wrongly accused inmates. This man knew the real murderer, and he
helped McCloskey find witnesses willing to corroborate the story.
Those familiar with the truth started coming forward, and McCloskey
was able to develop a compelling body of evidence that pointed to
Baker's innocence.

"We like to think our investigations are as complete as they could
be," he says. "The hub of the wheel is vindication. The spokes go to
the witnesses to see if they would come forward. Another spoke is

documentation. Another is forensics and testing of evidence. You have to develop every aspect of the case and not focus only on one."

McCloskey was certain he had developed every aspect of the Baker case, and a December 1996 evidentiary hearing convinced him that Eddie Baker would soon be a free man. But the judge's decision about ordering a new trial, promised in January, was postponed until April, then postponed again two more times. By late August, McCloskey's patience seemed to be exhausted. "I can't wait for that date," he wearily said in his Princeton, New Jersey, office a week before the scheduled hearing. "I just can't wait."

The following Thursday, McCloskey's years of painstaking work appeared to have finally paid off: A Common Pleas Court judge branded Baker's 1974 conviction a "miscarriage of justice" and granted the accused murderer a new trial. McCloskey began making arrangements to have Baker released on bail, and Baker's family planned a party to celebrate his homecoming. But a last-minute court ruling ordered that Baker be kept behind bars until the district attorney's appeal of the new-trial decision was heard.

The waiting was still not over.

It's not difficult to figure out what motivated James C. McCloskey. One wall of his office is covered with photos of those he's helped free from prison. A framed John Adams quote reads, in part: "It [is] more beneficial that many guilty persons should escape unpunished than one innocent person should suffer." There is a photo of a Southern lynching and another of Jackie Robinson in his Brooklyn Dodgers uniform. There is also a rock atop a file cabinet engraved with the single word "Question."

McCloskey seems to question everything. In the mid-1970s, he shocked friends and family by abruptly abandoning a successful business career to enroll in Princeton Theological Seminary. Before being ordained as a Presbyterian minister, he left the seminary to work full-time on winning the freedom of an inmate he believed had been wrongly convicted of murder. The process took a year, but McCloskey prevailed. And when he learned of another lifer wrongly imprisoned, McCloskey knew he'd found his life's work. Centurion Ministries was soon born.

McCloskey and his small staff, which is supported by a team of volunteers, practice a unique brand of muckraking. After all, their efforts to unearth facts and dredge up truths could have life-or-death consequences.

The process starts with a careful review of inmates' letters. Pleas that meet Centurion's criteria—those from death-row prisoners, for example—are set aside for further investigation. The staff collects information about each case, searching for clues that may reveal whether the letter writer was in fact wrongly convicted. The entire written record of a case is reviewed. The inmate is interviewed at length. His character is assessed; his version of the facts is analyzed. If a case has particular merit, Centurion orders trial transcripts for study. "The only thing we care about," McCloskey says, "is, based on a long but objective study of the case, plus a subjective evaluation of the individual, do we believe the person is completely innocent of the crime?"

Proving that innocence is, of course, another matter. Sometimes, McCloskey admits, he simply gets lucky. But most of the time, he explains, success requires something more predictable: "It takes good old shoe leather."

For McCloskey, that means doing whatever it takes to ferret out answers, although "whatever it takes" changes from one case to another. "There's no formula," he says.

There is, however, a distinct psychological approach that's inevitably part of the methodology. "It's like the turtle and the hare," McCloskey says. "We're the turtle. We plod along, inch along. To do this work, you have to take the long-term view. If not, you'll go crazy."

That long-term view has McCloskey and his investigators combing through every piece of paper they can find, knocking on every single door that may yield information. McCloskey won't tape-record people without their knowledge; only once in seventeen years has he followed someone. Instead, he doggedly searches for eyewitnesses and then tries to cajole them with his powers of persuasion. "You're trying to convince people to do the right thing," he says. "You appeal to their innermost moral core."

This unorthodox approach has paid dividends for McCloskey, who sometimes plies his trade in his cleric's collar. For example, he once tracked down a man who was threatened with imprisonment if he didn't lie and testify against McCloskey's client. The witness recanted his testimony to McCloskey and even visited the prison to apologize to the man he'd helped falsely imprison for a decade.

"I ask people to do what I'm not sure I'd have the courage to do," McCloskey adds.

But even when McCloskey finds witnesses willing to set the record straight, he may still face frustrating roadblocks. Consider the Eddie Baker case: The district attorney appealed the ruling to free Baker on bail, and the higher court sided with the government. The party to celebrate Baker's freedom was unexpectedly postponed.

That revocation of bail was in turn appealed to the Pennsylvania Supreme Court, but a month and a half later Baker, McCloskey, and everyone else involved in the drama were still awaiting a decision. McCloskey feared that Baker might end up incarcerated for another year or two while the appeals process played out.

But McCloskey was philosophical. There is, after all, a board in his office that displays another fourteen cases under active investigation. One on the list is a death-row inmate from Tyler, Texas; the others are lifers scattered from Baltimore to St. Louis to Oklahoma City. Another Philadelphia man McCloskey is helping has been in prison since 1964.

McCloskey says that having multiple projects to occupy his attention is of great value. "When I'm waiting for something to happen and having frustration," he says, "I'm working on other things."

For the moment, he is focused on the case of a prisoner in New Iberia, Louisiana. McCloskey is frustrated, but he knows the feeling goes with the job. "It's a roller-coaster ride," he says. "There's nothing you can do but just wait."

Open for Business

Like the federal government, each state has its own "sunshine" laws. In essence, these laws guarantee the public's right of access to governmental meetings and records. State freedom-of-information acts or their equivalents provide access to documents, while open-meeting laws permit the public to monitor the activities of state and local boards, commissions, agencies, and other governing bodies. Private corporations aren't covered by such laws, so you shouldn't show up at a company's board meeting expecting to waltz in and get the lowdown on its secrets.

Although every state has sunshine laws, some legislatures have put a higher priority on public access to information than have their counterparts elsewhere. These laws are clearly laid out in the state statutes, but that doesn't necessarily mean all the bureaucrats will be familiar with the details. Therefore, you need to know your rights.

The state attorney general's office will be able to answer questions about the particulars of the law. Here are some key areas worth exploring:

- Must officials allot a portion of each meeting for questions from the public? If a public official has been dodging your phone calls, for example, this may be your chance to put her on the spot.

- If the public is entitled to attend the meetings of boards and commissions, what exactly constitutes a "meeting"? In some states, two or more members of the same board discussing matters that may come before that body for action fits the definition. You may not have known about the meeting, and therefore didn't attend, but notes from that tête-à-tête may be available for your inspection. Find out if a quorum is required for the meeting to be deemed official.

- What agencies are covered by the state's sunshine laws? Unlike the federal sunshine law, some state laws also require that certain legislative and judicial bodies conduct their business in public. But what about meetings of publicly funded university trustees? And what about a meeting of the school's deans? In some states, even nongovernmental groups may fall under the sunshine law if they're supported by public funds or use public facilities. There have been court rulings in each state examining who is subject to the open-meetings law, and you may find that meetings you assumed were closed are in fact open.

- If the law requires that minutes of state and local meetings be taken, are these records public? If so, must a Freedom of

Information Act request be filed, or may you simply show up at the appropriate office and request to see the minutes?

- How much public notice must be given of a meeting, and where must it be published? If you suspect that a local commission may try to rule on a matter without a full public airing, make sure to learn the public-notice requirements.

- What constitutes a "public record"? Meeting minutes are usually public, but are copies of photographs, tape recordings, and computer files collected by that board or commission also available? If so, what are the fees that the board may legally charge you? Similarly, if the meeting itself is taped, find out if a copy of that is also available for purchase.

- Are board and agency members-elect subject to sunshine laws? If these new members are briefed on pending matters by sitting board members, you may be entitled to notes from the meetings.

- Is it legal to videotape a meeting? If so, a videotape could provide you with a valuable form of documentation if a public official goes back on his or her word. (For tips on using video to document your investigation, see Chapter Eight.)

- Under what circumstances may a board or commission bar the public from its meetings? There are usually some matters that may be considered "behind closed doors." These might include discussions of collective-bargaining negotiations or an ongoing lawsuit, for example. If an agency decrees that the meeting is closed, ask for an explanation. If you're not satisfied, formally register your objection by asking that it be read into the minutes. Document who barred you from the meeting, and ask that the denial be put in writing. Be aware that in some states, a government official who illegally bars the public from a meeting may be liable for criminal or civil fines. If you believe you were illegally barred, consult with the attorney general's office about the appeals process.

The following are phone numbers and, where available, Web sites for state attorneys general:

Alabama   (334) 242-7300   www.ago.state.al.us

Alaska	(907) 465-3600	www.law.state.ak.us/ag.html
Arizona	(602) 542-4266	www.attorneygeneral.state.az.us
Arkansas	(501) 682-1323	www.ag.state.ar.us
California	(916) 445-9555	caag.state.ca.us
Colorado	(303) 866-4500	**www.state.co.us/gov_dir/dol/index.htm**
Connecticut	(860) 808-5318	www.cslnet.ctstateu.edu/attygenl
Delaware	(302) 577-8300	www.state.de.us/attgen/index.htm
D. C.	(202) 727-6248	
Florida	(850) 487-1963	legal.firn.edu
Georgia	(404) 656-3300	www.ganet.org/ago
Hawaii	(808) 586-1282	www.hawaii.gov/ag/index.html
Idaho	(208) 334-2400	www.state.id.us/ag/home-page.htm
Illinois	(217) 782-1090	www.ag.state.il.us
Indiana	(317) 232-6201	www.state.in.us/hoosier advocate
Iowa	(515) 281-5164	www. state.ia.us/government/ag/index.html
Kansas	(785) 296-2215	www.ink.org/public/ksag
Kentucky	(502) 696-5300	www.law.state.ky.us
Louisiana	(504) 342-7013	www.laag.com/home.cfm

Maine	(207) 626-8800	www.state.me.us/ag /homepage.htm
Maryland	(410) 576-6300	www.oag.state.md.us
Massachusetts	(617) 727-2200	www.magnet.state.ma.us /ag
Michigan	(517) 373-1110	www.ag.state.mi.us
Minnesota	(651) 296-6196	www.ag.state.mn.us/home /mainhi.shtml
Mississippi	(601) 359-3680	www.ago.state.ms.us
Missouri	(573) 751-3321	www.ago.state.mo.us /index.htm
Montana	(406) 444-2026	www.doj.mt.gov/ago /index.htm
Nebraska	(402) 471-2682	www.nol.org/home/ago
Nevada	(775) 687-4170	www.state.nv.us/ag
New Hampshire	(603) 271-3658	www.state.nh.us/nhdoj /index.html
New Jersey	(609) 292-8740	www.state.nj.us/lps
New Mexico	(505) 827-6000	www.ago.state.nm.us
New York	(518) 474-7330	www.oag.state.ny.us
North Carolina	(919) 716-6400	www.jus.state.nc.us
North Dakota	(701) 328-2210	www.state.nd.us/ndag /index.html
Ohio	(614) 466-3376	www.ag.ohio.gov
Oklahoma	(405) 521-3921	www.oag.state.ok.us /oagweb.nsf
Oregon	(503) 378-6002	www.doj.state.or.us
Pennsylvania	(717) 787-3391	www.attorneygeneral.gov

Rhode Island	(401) 274-4400	www.riag.state.ri.us
South Carolina	(803) 734-3970	www.scattorneygeneral.org
South Dakota	(605) 773-3215	www.state.sd.us/state /executive/attorney /attorney.html
Tennessee	(615) 741-6474	www.attorneygeneral.state. tn.us
Texas	(512) 463-2100	www.oag.state.tx.us
Utah	(801) 538-9600	attygen.state.ut.us
Vermont	(802) 828-3171	www.state.vt.us/atg
Virginia	(804) 786-2071	www.oag.state.va.us
Washington	(360) 753-6200	www.wa.gov/ago
West Virginia	(304) 558-2021	www.state.wv.us/wvag
Wisconsin	(608) 266-1221	www.doj.state.wi.us
Wyoming	(307) 777-7841	www.state.wy.us/~ag /index.html

The Art of the Interview

Information is of no value if you can't pry it loose from someone. Unfortunately, inexperienced muckrakers often leave interviews empty-handed, because their subjects simply won't spill the beans.

Ken Metzler, author of *Creative Interviewing* (third edition, Allyn & Bacon, 1997), can help. According to Metzler, whose book is loaded with valuable interviewing techniques, the best journalistic interviewers have three traits in common: curiosity, listening ability, and tolerance for varying views and opinions. Whatever your traits, says Metzler, these suggestions will help:

- **Know what an interview is.** A journalistic interview is a conversation between two people to elicit factual information (including opinion and comment) on behalf of an unseen audience. A more sophisticated definition would suggest an "exchange" of information. The more information the interviewer brings to the conversation through experience or preparation, the better the interview will go.

- **Have a clear and preferably altruistic purpose for your interview.** Explain that purpose to your respondent. Be specific: "I want to write a detailed and anecdotal case history of your experiences as a foot-patrol officer in Central Park, with an emphasis on violent crime." You may have to sell the altruism: "If citizens know more about park violence, they'll be better prepared." These explanations solve problems such as the often-voiced interviewer complaint, "My subject keeps straying off target." Your respondent probably never knew the target in the first place: It was never explained.

- **Prepare.** For an important interview, consult documents, search for pertinent literature, conduct preliminary interviews—in short, do your homework much as you would prepare for an exam.

- **Listen—and do so nonjudgmentally.** Show that you're listening by eye contact, smiles, nods, "uh-huhs," and occasionally repeating your understanding of the respondent's points. Nonjudgmental listening means letting the person say what he or she really thinks and feels. You need not agree. But even the pariahs of society may have something worthwhile to contribute to the public good and should be appreciated for doing so. Keep an open mind.

- **Use your mental "down time" effectively.** Your mind runs three to four times faster than people's speech, so you can tune in and out of the conversation. You can use that non-listening time to evaluate what is said, take notes, make comparisons with other data, and think up new questions.

- **Probe.** Ask follow-up questions. The answer to your first question on a topic probably is not important; it's more likely to lead to further questions and answers until you get to the nub of the matter via questions you didn't know you were going to ask.

- **Conduct your interview in a logical pattern.** One is chronological ("Start at the beginning and take me through the sequence of events"); another is bottom line first ("Please tell me some of your accomplishments over the years, starting with the one you're most proud of"). Another pattern bears the acronym GOSS—Goals, Obstacles, Solutions, Start. Those worthy of being interviewed have goals, but obstacles stand in the way of the goals, although solutions have been found or are contemplated. The final "S" is for start: Inquire about how the situation or event began. GOSS works because news articles tend to focus on events, including setbacks, in the Quest for Achievement by newsworthy people and agencies.

- **Keep the interview conversational.** Start with icebreakers: Talk of weather or mutual acquaintances or news events—just as real people do. Casual conversation often takes capricious turns and reverses that may upset your interview pattern. Yet interviews that follow those caprices often produce unguarded and insightful answers. So depart from your interview pattern as the conversation dictates, but be thankful you have a pattern so you'll know how to return to it.

- **Use flattery.** If you hear a quotable quote or anything else you find useful, make an agreeable fuss about how much you enjoyed it. You'll be surprised how often you receive more of the same now that your respondent understands what you want. Clever questions are less effective than encouraging responses.

- **Be alert.** Research suggests that our mental faculties are aided by rest, physical exercise, and good nourishment, and are dulled by alcohol, drugs (legal or not), fatigue, and preoccupation with irrelevancies. With alert mental faculties, we are able to listen between the lines to catch nuances of meaning or things only half-articulated.

Affairs of State

The number of publicly accessible records maintained by state and local agencies can seem almost endless. Consider, for example, some of the files available from South Carolina's Department of Labor,

Licensing, and Regulation: Office of Elevators and Amusement Rides Inspection accident investigation summaries; Division of Fire and Life Safety licensing and complaint files; Office of Occupational Safety and Health imminent-danger citations; Office of Migrant Labor files. The list goes on and on.

Searching such records can be a daunting task. Fortunately, an increasing number of governmental agencies are providing electronic access to their records—a particularly valuable aid for tracking down people, their associates, their assets, and their personal histories. Nora Paul, of the Florida-based Poynter Institute for Media Studies (www.poynter.org, 888-POYNTER, or 727-821-9494), has compiled a valuable guide to the ins and outs of using public-records databases for such purposes—including both the advantages and the pitfalls. The first section explores the types of records available, what these records can provide, and search parameters to help you get the information you need. Some databases are statewide. Others are local compilations, meaning that full coverage would require a county-by-county search.

The Paper Chase

Motor-vehicle information: automobile registrations, driver's licenses, accident reports.

- Can provide address, date of birth, driver history, Social Security number (in some states), physical characteristics of the driver (height, weight, race, sex, need for eyeglasses), type of automobile driven (make, model, year).

- Necessary to search by name (sometimes full name and date of birth are required), driver's-license number, vehicle identification number (VIN), or motor-vehicle registration number.

Secretary of State filings: incorporation records, uniform commercial code filings, limited partnerships.

- Can provide address information, names of business associates and associated businesses, name of the company's registered agent, address of the business, status of the business, names of debtors and creditors.

- Necessary to search by name of officer or business name.

Property records: tax appraisals and mortgage filings.

- Can provide name and address of owner, characteristics of the house (square feet, number of rooms), mortgage holder and amount, appraised value, who sold the house and when.
- Necessary to search by address of the property, owner's or seller's name.

Utility records: water and sewer billings.

- Can provide name and address of owner (useful for rented properties), delinquency of payment.
- Necessary to search by property address, owner's name.

Voter registration records.

- Can provide address information, party affiliation, last election he or she voted.
- Necessary to search by person's name.

Marriage/divorce records.

- Can provide maiden name of bride, dates of marriage/divorce, whether there were previous marriages.
- Necessary to search by name.

Occupational licenses.

- Can provide information about business line, address.
- Necessary to search by name.

Civil and criminal court cases/criminal history.

- Can provide plaintiff's and defendant's names, lawyers' names, case-file numbers (to get the full case record), arrest records.
- Need to search by name, case number.

Other records of interest: concealed-weapons permits, boat and aircraft registrations, bankruptcy filings, mortgage default records.

Ways Agency Databases Are Made Available

Direct access to the agency's computer, such as a dial-in account to Department of Motor Vehicle records.

Advantage: The data is as current as the agency has available.

Disadvantages: Sometimes the search interface is not designed for consumer use and is not user-friendly. It is possible the agency can monitor what is being searched on the database. Sometimes the database is available only during regular office hours.

Gateway through a commercial database vendor such as CompuServe.

Advantage: Same as above: You are getting exactly what the agency has available.

Disadvantages: Same as above, plus there is usually an additional charge for online search time.

Agency sells database to a vendor, which repackages it for commercial use.

Advantages: The database is more consumer-oriented and usually easier to search. There is often a wide range of databases available (by type of record or geographic area), providing one-stop shopping for public records. Some services pull records together, providing a dossier of the person you are looking for. Usually, there is round-the-clock access to the records.

Disadvantages: Records are often not as current as those in the agency's database, and all counties in a state database may not be represented. A premium is paid for access to the data, perhaps making it the more expensive option.

Through a bulletin-board service. Federal appellate courts, trial courts, and bankruptcy courts offer bulletin-board dial-in service to case and docket information. There is a central registration number (800-676-6856). More information is available online about Public Access to Court Electronic Records (PACER): pacer.psc.uscourts.gov.

Advantages: Fairly inexpensive; some districts are free. Does not require a high-end computer for access.

Disadvantages: Separate access to the different courts; no centralized call-in. Courts have their electronic bulletin boards arranged differently.

On the Internet. The University of Kentucky has put the state's Vital Records Index on the Web. It contains various death, marriage, and divorce records. Hopefully, more such university/agency collaborations will follow.

Advantages: It's free. Quick and easy search template. Provides basic information (age, race, county of residence, and date of event).

Disadvantage: The search is by name only.

Locator service companies subscribe to various public-records databases and offer comprehensive search and retrieval of records in both electronic and paper forms.

Advantages: Subscriptions to a number of services isn't necessary. Service companies can access records in a number of forms through a network of searchers in various cities.

Disadvantages: Probably the most costly option because users are billed for the cost of the search plus a service charge. Quick turnaround service usually costs extra; there may be several days' delay getting some records.

Purchase tapes of the data and access on your own computer.

Advantages: No cost for searching after the data has been purchased. The data can run on software that is designed for easy use.

Disadvantage: If database updates are frequent, the purchased database is quickly outdated.

How to Locate Public-Records Databases

Not all state or local governments offer the same level of access to similar records. Likewise, not all records of the same type have the same information from state to state. (New York, for example, does not require the listing of officers' names in corporate filings, while other states do.) Some public-records search companies are offering more comprehensive access to records, although the compilation of most local-level records is not yet a reality. Here are some ways to track down public records for your state and local area:

- **Check with the agency itself.** Determine which agencies' files you would find useful for routine checks (corporate filings, drivers' records, and property records are generally the most useful). Call the agency's data manager to see whether direct access is possible.

- **Check with public-records database vendors.** Several database vendors specialize in public-records access. Shop around to see which have the types of records you want and the most comprehensive coverage.

- **Check with a university data center.** Many large universities have data centers with tape libraries of state data. They can tell you the availability status of different records.

- **Check with the state information center or the city/county data-processing office.** These are the keepers of the information inventory. They will know what databases are available and what records are accessible.

Maintaining Order

You've spent a week in the library photocopying newspaper and magazine articles about a company suspected of wrongdoing. You've ordered articles of incorporation and annual reports from the secretary of state. You've downloaded hundreds of pages about the firm off the Internet, and a Freedom of Information Act request has yielded thousands more pages. You have depositions from court cases, interview notes from former employees, license applications from state regulatory agencies, and various public filings obtained from the Securities and Exchange Commission. In short, you've compiled a file cabinet's worth of incredible information, and now for the report you're writing you desperately need some facts you saw buried in one of the documents. But which one?

Gathering data may be an art, but cataloging it is a science. Unfortunately, it's a discipline that few novices pay attention to—at least until they go looking for that elusive piece of paper.

So before you get buried in documents, it's wise to institute a logical filing and indexing system that will let you quickly retrieve names, dates, and anything else of interest. As many frustrated veterans will testify, a stack of file cards usually won't cut it. Instead, the searching power afforded by a computer is critical.

There are many systems that make use of the microchip. Here's a simple yet effective one that's been passed among some of the best investigative journalists.

- Compile a list of subjects and label file folders accordingly. Some subject files will be immediately obvious. For example, if you're investigating a company believed to be exposing its workers to asbestos, you'll immediately know that your research will include background on (a) the company, (b) its directors, and (c) asbestos. As the research continues, you may create new files for company subsidiaries, lawsuits against the firm, government studies, and so on.

- As documents are collected, each is assigned its own unique identifier number that's keyed to subject files. For example, each document related to a lawsuit may be labeled with "LAW" and a three-digit number, while materials about the directors are labeled "DIR" and a number. So the first newspaper article you find with information about the directors might be assigned DIR001, which is written in an upper corner of the reprint for easy identification. The next document you turn up about the directors, be it another article or a company news release, would be labeled DIR002 and written in that same corner of the page.

- Key information on each document is marked with a yellow highlighter. If a Freedom of Information Act request yields a document that includes the name of a company whistleblower, highlight it. If it also includes references to a study on asbestos workers in this particular industry, highlight that, too.

- All pertinent information is then entered on the computer. A database program will allow you to sort the information later, making it easy to quickly find everything that refers to an individual, for instance. You can, however, use a word processor with this system. First enter a document's unique identifier. Next add the subject heading (for example, "Lawsuit, XYZ Corp., Asbestos Studies"). After that add all highlighted names, numbers, town names, dates, and so on. Keep it short; this isn't the place to include an entire sentence describing an asbestos-related condition, but rather a keyword such as the condition itself. Separate each field of data with a tab.

- After entering the data, place each document in the appropriate folder, in numerical order. If you ever remove a document from a folder, return it to its proper place when you're finished.

- Assume you've amassed a thousand documents that have been cataloged in 40 file folders. Now assume you want all documents that include something about the company president. You may have created a file with his name on it, but he may also have been mentioned in newspaper articles that are scattered in files on the company, lawsuits, and a dozen other subjects. Simply search for his name and record the corresponding identifier numbers. You'll know which files to remove from the drawer and exactly where in each file to look.

The key to this system is to highlight all the keywords that you may want to find later. That means some extra work on the front end, but it also means that you won't be futilely digging through knee-deep mounds of paper.

Muckraking 101
Lesson Two: Getting Up to Speed

There are many questions that need answering, but all seem to hinge on these: Who is this animal dealer who has aroused curiosity, and what exactly is his arrangement with the city-run zoo?

At the board meeting, the director of the Ebbinger Zoo revealed this much: The man's name is Timothy Overpeck, and he lives in the town of Martinson. That may not be much to go on, but it's a start. The **public library** has a statewide collection of **telephone books**, one of which turns up Overpeck's address and phone number. A **map** shows that he lives on the outskirts of Martinson, which is described in a **state almanac** as a sparsely populated farming community. Running the address in a **crisscross directory** turns up a second phone number—this one for something called Animal Express. A call to the Lemke **County clerk's office** reveals that the actual name of the business is Timothy's Animal Express. An employee of the **secretary of state's corporation division** finds the company in the agency's computers, which yields the names and addresses of the officers, directors, and registered agent. Every document may hold some clue, so an order is placed for the **articles of incorporation, amendments filed to the articles, and the most recent annual report**. These documents will go into folders, while notes of every conversation—with names, dates, and phone numbers—are **logged in a notebook**.

The reference specialist at the Lemke **County Library** finds nothing about Timothy's Animal Express in the **vertical files**. The **Better Business Bureau** has not received any complaints. There is no listing in a **directory of the state's major businesses**.

Because Overpeck is an animal dealer, he probably needs some sort of **license**. A local animal warden cannot provide any answers. But a **compendium of the state's laws** says that a permit from the Department of Natural Resources is required to own, sell, barter, or propagate wild animals. **The government blue book** lists all the DNR phone extensions, and a call to the **office of public information** at the capitol confirms that Timothy Overpeck has a valid propagator's license. The DNR official says that Overpeck also has a federal license, issued by the U.S Department of Agriculture. So far, everything the zoo director said is checking out. This is shaping up to be a wild-goose chase.

But the investigation continues nonetheless. *The United States Government Manual* lists a phone number for a local field office of the Department of Agriculture. An employee there says that responsibility for issuing dealer permits lies with the USDA's Animal and Plant Health Inspection Service (APHIS), whose headquarters are outside Washington, D.C. A call to the **Office of Public Information** confirms that Tim Overpeck has a federal Class C license. When asked to explain this license, the APHIS official says that it's issued to those primarily engaged in exhibiting animals. So Overpeck is not a dealer after all, but apparently runs a zoo of some sort.

A call to the Lemke County **Chamber of Commerce** reveals that there are no zoos in the county. Another call to the state **Department of Natural Resources** confirms this. Something isn't adding up, so a list of all the nation's Class C exhibitors is retrieved from the **APHIS Web site**. Bingo: Timothy Overpeck also owns the Wildest Things Animal Park in Schuyler, just across the state line.

The **search for records is repeated**, the phone numbers this time fished from *Carroll's State Directory*. A call to the **neighboring state's DNR** confirms that Tim Overpeck is the proprietor of Wildest Things and is licensed to import and display wild animals. A clerk in the **Secretary of State's office** gives out instructions for ordering documents. The phone number for the Schuyler Public Library comes from an old standby—**directory assistance**. A **librarian** says she has a file for the petting zoo and agrees to retrieve it. There is a **brochure** in the folder, she says, and a single **article** from the *Schuyler Standard*— something about Wildest Things being fined by the government. "Would you like a copy?" she asks.

Indeed you would.

Next: The Paper Chase

CHAPTER FOUR

Local Heroes

*When a mighty Texas utility decided to build a nuclear power plant
near Dallas, nothing appeared to be standing in its way. But out of
a nearby neighborhood appeared Juanita Ellis, who showed the corporate bigwigs what power is really all about, and who showed
others waging local battles how to outflank the competition.*

The turning point in Juanita Ellis's battle against the licensing of
Comanche Peak nuclear power plant wasn't a court order or
a regulatory-agency decision or the release of confidential documents unearthed by a Freedom of Information Act request. Rather, it
was simply an unlikely phrase uttered during an out-of-the-blue phone
call.

It was the summer of 1982, nearly a decade into Ellis's fight to
expose what she believed were potential safety problems with the
reactor under construction in the rocky hills near Dallas. Ellis's interest in the issue had been piqued by a magazine article detailing the
lack of adequate insurance at nuclear power plants, and it was subsequently fueled by the revelation that the Dallas City Council had
scheduled hearings on an operating permit for Comanche Peak without notifying the community. Thus began a grueling, uphill fight for
Ellis, a plant-nursery worker with no background in physics, engi-
neering, or any other discipline that might qualify her as a
nuclear-power expert.

But what Ellis lacked in credentials she made up for in savvy,
research skills, and sheer determination. Add to that a committed
band of cohorts known as Citizens for Safe Energy (CASE), whose
original membership included just six names, and Ellis somehow

managed to forestall the plans of the very well-heeled—and politically well-connected—Texas Utilities Electric Company. It was never easy, however.

"Our two biggest opponents were the Nuclear Regulatory Commission and the Texas Utilities staffs," she recalls. "We had to fight tooth and nail just to get documents."

Such stonewalling spurred Ellis to try other research means. She attended public hearings, for example, where she demanded answers about plant safety and other pertinent matters. All evidence presented by Texas Utilities in its defense was in turn passed along to CASE, giving the community group essential details about the design of the nuclear reactor. Such information proved valuable, but the turning point in Ellis's crusade came only when a former employee of Comanche Peak turned whistleblower. In a phone call to Ellis, engineer Mark Walsh expressed concern about the plant's technical design—specifically, the instability of pipe supports, which he claimed could lead to a collapse.

"I remember he called and was talking about his having worked at the plant, and quit the plant, and was very concerned about it," Ellis recalls. "He said they didn't even know about strudel. And I thought, Boy we've really got a live one here, talking about cooking."

In fact, the "strudel" that Ellis's tipster referred to was STRUDEL, an acronym for "structural design language," the computer program used at Comanche Peak. This unsolicited call came as CASE was preparing its testimony for a licensing-board hearing, and its hopes at the time were pinned on government and utility-company documents that, in truth, did little to bolster the group's antinuclear agenda. But Ellis suddenly realized that she'd found someone with the sort of technical, insider knowledge that would be meaningful to the licensing board. To her glee, Walsh then put Ellis in touch with a disgruntled colleague who had also resigned from Comanche Peak.

Other whistleblowers had previously come forth, but they typically spoke to matters that reflected only their plant experience; now CASE had as allies a pair of engineers familiar with a wide array of pertinent issues—expertise that eventually helped the group gain the upper hand against Texas Utilities. In fact, the two engineers were later hired on as consultants to CASE.

"I guess I kind of held it all together," says Ellis, referring to the logistics of the battle. "But as far as the technical issues which we had to deal with, I certainly couldn't have done it without expert help."

That decision to enlist outside experts proved to be critical, as the whistleblowers-turned-consultants helped poke holes in studies of plant safety presented during licensing hearings. But it was only one of many valuable lessons learned by Ellis over the course of her campaign.

Battling a local entity—be it a utility, a police department, or a government agency—may call for a variety of different strategies. In the Northern Virginia suburbs of Washington, D.C., for instance, taxpayer groups unhappy with pension deals for county executives sued to have the retirement plan nullified. A Dallas-area citizen used the Freedom of Information Act to obtain videotapes that showed a police officer apparently spraying pepper gas at a woman in a holding cell; after a local TV station aired segments, the officer was suspended. Illinois residents unhappy with the way a local airport was being governed undertook a yearlong study that used public records to prove its contentions.

For Ellis's group, becoming formally involved in public hearings proved to be a key first step. By being officially designated as an intervenor in the hearings process, CASE was entitled to ask questions of the power company, the utility commission, and other interested parties. To be granted intervenor status, CASE successfully demonstrated that it had "standing"—that is, it showed that one of its members lived close enough to the power plant to be harmed by an accident. Being afforded such status proved crucial, because it gave the group access to internal reports and decisions that would not otherwise have been available. Of course, the privilege cut both ways: The antinuclear group was also forced to answer a barrage of its opponents' interrogatories, which at times, Ellis claims, felt like harassment.

Prior to the operating-license hearings, it was difficult to generate community interest in the power plant. CASE published newsletters and issued press releases, but the former was time-consuming and the latter were largely ignored. Eventually, Ellis more or less gave up on using news releases to pique media interest.

But the hearings generated that interest, in turn bringing calls from reporters. And the 1979 debacle at Three Mile Island generated a flood of inquiries from the local media. "I could put them in touch with somebody, and I think that really established our credibility better than anything else had in the past," says Ellis. "Over a period of time, some of the reporters got to know me, and they knew we could back up what we were saying. The utility could make broad statements and get away with it, but we had to prove everything we told them."

Ellis relied primarily on three sources for her information—the Nuclear Regulatory Commission, Texas Utilities, and whistleblowers. She could seek documents from the NRC via the Freedom of Information Act, and the discovery process that was granted CASE as an intervenor made power-company materials accessible. But cultivating whistleblowers was a wait-and-hope exercise. Fortunately, positive media coverage made CASE easy to find, bringing a regular stream of calls from disgruntled Texas Utilities employees with first-hand information. In-person meetings were arranged, and CASE then followed up on the tips with requests for the pertinent documents.

When Ellis attended licensing hearings, she'd raise new concerns based on the whistleblowers' statements and the documents she had subsequently accumulated. To consider these issues, the NRC licensing board scheduled additional hearings. In fact, the hearings dragged on for four years, delaying even further the utility company's plans and driving up the cost by billions of dollars.

Fighting Texas Utilities became such an all-consuming task that Ellis finally quit her job. In the midst of the hearings, she filed a 446-page document with the NRC outlining her findings about the cost and safety issues at Comanche Peak. Inside sources later told her that the document became known to NRC regulators as the "Yellow Bomb."

When the smoke from that incendiary ream of paper finally cleared, Ellis and her group had gained the upper hand. The licensing board conceded that too many important issues had been raised, and it put everything on hold while Texas Utilities worked on redesign and reconstruction plans. To resolve the impasse, the company also brought in new management. William Counsil was put in charge of the project, and one of his first decisions was to meet with Ellis.

"He called me up and took a whole different approach," says Ellis. "After meeting at a restaurant, which was neutral territory, he even transferred boxes of documents from his trunk to mine."

For the first time, meetings were convened between engineers on both sides of the contentious struggle. Town meetings were convened. Texas Utilities not only provided CASE with documents it requested, but the company also honestly addressed its adversary's concerns. Over the next three years, in fact, CASE and the power company's new managers overhauled the plant's design. The citizen group was even allowed to inspect the plant at each stage of development.

In 1988, Ellis was appointed to a five-year stint on Comanche Peak's oversight board. In addition, CASE was given the right to be present for quality inspection audits and to ask questions during the process. It was also awarded a monetary settlement for its debts and to keep its work going forward. In return, CASE dropped its objections to the licensing of the nuclear reactor.

Some antinuclear groups branded the settlement a sellout—a pitfall of the muckraking process that Ellis never anticipated. But she's nonetheless happy with the outcome and pleased with the process, which she admits worked better than she had ever imagined.

"One point I'd really like to get across," she says, "is that it's a lot of work, but you don't have to be a nuclear scientist to make a difference and do something. You really don't. Anyone who can think and read can do a lot."

Unturned Stones

Muckraking 101, lesson three, which follows on page 78, offers a seemingly hypothetical quest to unearth truths about transactions at a local zoo. But many of the methods outlined in the six-part series that unfolds throughout these pages illustrates actual techniques used by Alan Green, Center for Public Integrity writer and author of *Animal Underworld: Inside America's Black Market for Rare and Exotic Species*.

Green's four-year investigation of the exotic-animal trade in the United States literally took him on a cross-country search for documents: He personally visited twenty-seven state capitals and hired researchers in other states to dig out paperwork that may help piece together the truth about sales of exotic species. In addition, Green filed many Freedom of Information Act requests, he interviewed hundreds of sources, he pored over mountains of documents, and he built a series of databases—one with more than seven thousand records—in his quest to shine a light on an industry that had historically conducted its affairs in secret.

Green has many practical tips about how to ferret out information, but he believes that the real key to muckraking is persistence—the determination to keep pursuing new avenues when roadblocks are thrown in your way. Throughout his career, Green says, he's met a number of successful citizen muckrakers, and the traits they share include resiliency, stubbornness, and unabashed determination. Green shares these traits, as well, as his recollection of the *Animal Underworld* reporting process demonstrates:

> The real turning point of my investigation into the trade in exotic animals came in late 1996, during a conversation with one of the few experts on the subject. After a year and a half of research, I had finally concluded that this was at its heart a story about laundering—a tale of how unwanted animals ("surplus," as they're called) owned by zoos, universities, and theme parks were sold and traded until their origins had been entirely obscured. That way, no one could identify with certainty the previous owners of an animal landing at an auction, a private hunting preserve, an exotic-meat butcher, or an abominable roadside attraction. The system of selling and reselling animals—passing them like relay batons from one dealer to another—insulated everyone involved from being identified as a party to this sordid commerce. There was, in short, deniability for all.
>
> Because much of my previous work as an investigative reporter had relied heavily on documents, I assumed that the veil of secrecy, which had frustrated other journalists, could be punctured by piecing together records from across the United States. So in this late-1996 discussion, I posed a question: Couldn't the truth be revealed, I asked, by going to every state capital to search out records, then methodically following the paper trails from location to location? "No," I was told. "It's not feasible."

"Why not?" I asked, certain that I had finally figured out a way to expose the well-guarded secrets of the exotic-animal industry.

"Because you'd have to go to every state capital. And who the heck is going to do that?"

A month later, I packed some maps and drove the first leg of what I soon came to think of as the Great Dome Tour.

All-Court Press

Finding cases of legal significance is relatively easy, since they're often "reported" in major indexes such as regional and federal digests (see page 35). But tracking down references to other cases—be they in state trial court or before a local magistrate—is not quite so simple; in fact, finding them is sometimes almost impossible. The reason: These cases are not cited in digests, nor are there references to most of them in the two major online legal databases, Lexis-Nexis and Westlaw. What's more, very small courts often have sketchy record-keeping systems. That means you're often fishing blindly, although there is nonetheless a methodical way to approach the search.

State Courts

The system of courts varies from state to state, although the basic structure is pyramidal in shape: At the lower level are the non-jury municipal courts (small claims, landlord-tenant, traffic), along with courts that handle various misdemeanors. Move up the pyramid, and the legal issues become more complex, the civil claims are for higher dollar amounts, and the criminal charges may result in prison. These trial courts, which typically include divorce and paternity cases, may also hear cases appealed from the lower-level courts or from administrative agencies. Keep moving to the pyramid's point, and you reach the appeals court and, ultimately, the state supreme court or its equivalent.

Although this is the typical structure of a state's court system, the names of the individual courts are often different. In Delaware, for example, alderman's courts and justice-of-the-peace courts are at the base of the pyramid; courts higher up the ladder include the court of common pleas, family court, superior court, and the court of chancery, whose jurisdiction includes matters related to corporate issues. In Tennessee, the pyramid moves from municipal courts (in some cities), juvenile courts (in some counties), and general sessions courts (in every county) to circuit courts, chancery courts, criminal courts in many of the state's judicial districts, and probate courts in two counties. Higher up are two appeals courts and the state supreme court.

This structure is important to remember, because an investigation may require that you search for court records in a number of states. Therefore, first make sure you know the name of each court and its jurisdiction. Any law library will have reference books that map out the organization of each state's judicial branch. An easy way to find this information online is via Courts.Net (www.courts.net), which provides links to all trial-level court home pages. Another top-flight resource for locating state-based legal (as well as regulatory) information is the Web site of Piper Resources, at www.piperinfo.com/state/states.html. Finally, Indiana University School of Law maintains a comprehensive state-government index that includes links to everything from local court directories to state bar associations. The address is www.law.indiana.edu/v-lib/ (then select "state government servers").

Finding cases at a local courthouse involves searching a database that lists the names of parties to lawsuits. Some courts have computerized the names, while others maintain them on microfiche, in ledger books, or in card catalogs. In some instances, you may need to search more than one index—a computerized listing for recent cases, for instance, and a card catalog for older cases.

When you find a plaintiff's or defendant's name in an index, copy the case docket number. Files for recent cases—including those still pending—will be housed at the courthouse, while files for older cases will be stored at a county records center or other archive. In both instances, you can request the case file by filling out a simple form.

A docket sheet will be attached to the file. This is your roadmap to the case; it will list, in chronological order, all actions that occurred, such as filings of motions and judges' orders. Request all the folders in the case file, but be forewarned that you may be inundated with documents. There may be hundreds of pages of depositions, for example; there may also be endless exhibits, such as canceled checks, phone records, and the like.

Because the clues you're after may be buried deep within those documents, plan a methodical search of the records. Court documents may be copied, but it's usually expensive—50 cents to a dollar per page is not unusual. Occasionally case records are sealed by the judge, so if you stumble across something of particular interest, don't wait to request a copy. If you do, it may later be sealed and therefore unavailable to you.

Remember that not every case filed ultimately goes to trial; many are settled before the courtroom showdown. But these cases will nonetheless be listed in the court index, and the dockets should be searched as well.

Also know that you don't necessarily have to search indexes in person. In some instances, case information is available by phone, mail, or even computer. But these methods may require contacting multiple courts, and it's possible that pertinent cases may be overlooked. One solution is to hire a document-search firm, which will scrutinize indexes and pull files from courts. To find such firms, try the *SourceBook of Local Court and County Record Retrievers* (BRB Publications). Alternatively, call the local bar association and ask for a referral.

Finally, be aware that searching local court records requires a well-planned strategy. One of the best sources for crafting such an attack is Dennis King's book *Get the Facts on Anyone, 3rd Edition* (Macmillan). In addition to court records, the book teaches the ins and outs of finding everything from pilot licenses to the salaries of top labor-union officials.

Federal Courts

The federal court system is also arranged like a pyramid. At the top is the Supreme Court of the United States, below which are the thirteen U.S. Courts of Appeals and the Court of Military Appeals. On the next level are 94 U.S. district courts and various specialized courts, including the Tax Court and the Court of International Trade. U.S. Bankruptcy Courts, also part of the federal judiciary, handle all bankruptcy proceedings for individuals and businesses.

While state and local courts handle most criminal proceedings and such day-to-day legal matters as contract disputes, probate of estates, and land dealings, the federal courts can decide criminal and civil cases brought under the U.S. Constitution or other federal laws, as well as some lawsuits between residents or corporations of different states.

References to federal cases are generally easier to find, because a higher proportion of them are "reported." Not all are reported, though, so don't assume that the absence of a name in a digest means that no court records exist.

Searching federal court records is much like searching state court records. One easy way to search is via PACER (Public Access to Court Electronic Records), which allows anyone with a personal computer to dial in to a district- or bankruptcy-court computer and retrieve case information and court dockets. A one-time registration is required, and users are then billed 60 cents per minute for online time. For information and registration, call the PACER Service Center at (800) 676-6856. Details are available on the Web site of the U.S. federal judiciary, at pacer.psc.uscourts.gov.

Archived cases end up in a federal records center. To view records housed in these repositories, you need specific information from the court, including the case-file name, the case-file number, and the federal-records-center location numbers. You'll also need to make an appointment to view the records.

The major federal centers that house court records are listed below. Each site also has records from federal agencies (but in some cases not covering precisely the same states as the court records). You can get details from the National Archives and Records Administration at the telephone numbers below or at www.nara.gov/regional.

NARA Northeast Region, 380 Trapelo Road, Waltham, MA 02452 (781-647-8104)
Areas served: Maine, Vermont, New Hampshire, Massachusetts, Connecticut, and Rhode Island

NARA Central Plains Region, 200 Space Center Drive, Lee's Summit, MO 64064 (816-478-7079)
Areas served: New York, New Jersey, Puerto Rico, and the U.S. Virgin Islands

NARA Mid-Atlantic Region, 14700 Townsend Road, Philadelphia, PA 19154 (215-671-9027)

Areas served: Delaware, Pennsylvania, Maryland, Virginia, and West Virginia

Washington National Records Center, 4205 Suitland Road, Suitland, MD 20746 (301-457-7000)

Area served: District of Columbia

NARA Southeast Region, 1557 St. Joseph Avenue, East Point, GA 30044 (404-763-7474)

Areas served: North Carolina, South Carolina, Tennessee, Mississippi, Alabama, Georgia, Florida, and Kentucky

NARA Great Lakes Region, 7358 South Pulaski Road, Chicago, IL 60629 (773-581-7816)

Areas served: Illinois, Wisconsin, Minnesota, Indiana, Michigan, and Ohio

NARA Central Plains Region, 2312 East Bannister Road, Kansas City, MO 64131 (816-926-6272)

Areas served: Kansas, Iowa, Nebraska, and Missouri

NARA Southwest Region, 501 W. Felix Street, Building 1, P.O. Box 6216, Fort Worth, TX 76115 (817-334-5525)

Areas served: Texas, Oklahoma, Arkansas, and Louisiana

NARA Rocky Mountain Region, Building 48, Denver Federal Center, P.O. Box 25307, Denver, CO 80225 (303-236-0804)

Areas served: Colorado, Wyoming, Utah, Montana, New Mexico, North Dakota, and South Dakota

NARA Pacific Region (San Francisco), 1000 Commodore Drive, San Bruno, CA 94066 (650-876-9009)

Areas served: Nevada (except Clark County), northern California, Hawaii, American Samoa, and the Pacific Trust Territories

NARA Pacific Region (Laguna Niguel), 24000 Avila Road, Laguna Niguel, CA 92677

P.O. Box 6719, Laguna Niguel, CA 92607 (949-360-2641)

Areas served: Arizona; Clark County, Nevada; and southern California

NARA Pacific Alaska Region, 6125 Sand Point Way NE, Seattle, WA 98115 (206-526-6501)

Areas served: Washington, Oregon, Idaho, and Alaska

What's Where

Getting your hands on federal government records can sometimes be a challenge, although the search can usually be narrowed quickly to the appropriate agency. Ditto state governments, even though jurisdiction may vary from one state to another. In most instances, for example, the Secretary of State has responsibility for matters related to elections, while in Alaska that responsibility falls to the lieutenant governor. But finding one's way through the thickets of county and local government records can be an unwelcome challenge, as researchers must contend with a panoply of agencies, departments, boards, and commissions.

So where to look? Here are some of the most likely sources of information about people and companies. Be advised that some jurisdictions may have prohibitions against making certain records public. If your request is turned down, ask that the denial be in writing and that it cite the appropriate law. In such instances, an appeal to the city attorney may prove fruitful.

Address	County tax collector
Annual report (private company) . .	Secretary of state, corporation division
Annual report (public company) . .	Federal Securities and Exchange Commission

Annual report (nonprofit)	Internal Revenue Service
Arrest records	Court clerk, criminal division
Articles of incorporation	Secretary of State, corporation division
Blueprints	Building inspector
Business licenses	City clerk
Cause of death	County coroner
County employee information	County auditor's office
Date of birth	County recorder, birth-certificates section
Divorce information	County clerk, divorce records
Easements	Surveyor's office
Health inspection record	Health department
Individual's photograph	Department of motor vehicles
Information on doctors	State licensing board
Jail confinement dates	Jail book
Maiden name.	County recorder, marriage-license section
Marital status	County clerk, marriage-license applications
Mortgages	County recorder
Name	Registrar of voters
Name changes	County clerk

Officials' cellular-phone records ...	City finance office
Plat records	City planning department
Political party	Registrar of voters
Probate actions	Court clerk, civil division
Property ownership (current)	Tax assessor's office
Property ownership (previous)	Recorder of deeds
Property taxes paid	County tax collector's office
Real-estate transactions	County recorder
Registered agent	Secretary of State, corporation division
Rights of way	Highway department
Tax liens	County clerk's office, civil files
Trade-name filings	County clerk
Uniform Commercial Code filings .	County recorder
Value of deceased's estate	Public administrator's office

Smooth Operators

There are 800 million pages of information on the Internet. Or maybe half that. Or is it twice as many?

No one knows for sure, but it's really immaterial. What matters is this: Is the data you need out there? And if so, will you be able to find it?

The same is true for online databases and CD-ROMs. Although these information products are powerful muckraking aides, they're of no value if your search strategy leaves you empty-handed. And a search that turns up a few thousand "hits" isn't of much value, either—unless you have a few spare months to kill.

The techniques of computer-assisted reporting, as outlined in the previous chapter, are in fact only useful to those with a well-designed game plan. Foraging for documents on the Internet is simplified by "search engines" such as Yahoo, Lycos, HotBot, or Alta Vista, but using these tools doesn't guarantee that you'll get what you need. And if your search turns up 50 great documents but fails to produce the one true "smoking gun" that's out there, then your efforts will by no means have been an unqualified success.

Each online service has its own search mechanism, as do the Internet search engines. What's more, each has its own strengths and weaknesses. For example, Alta Vista is ideal for finding scientific information on the Internet, while Excite offers excellent summaries of its hits and HotBot is ideal for name searches.

What's common to many of them, however, is that searchers may use so-called Boolean operators. Mastering the use of three simple terms—AND, OR, NOT—will give you a decided edge in your computer-assisted reporting.

Credit the nineteenth-century mathematician George Boole with Boolean logic, a form of algebra that reduces all values to either true or false. If your ninth-grade math has long since faded, you need only remember this: By using Boolean operators, your search will be tailored to find more precise results.

- **AND:** When you place the word AND between two specified terms, you're indicating that you only want records containing *both* of those keywords.

Search example: Vermont AND catamount

This means that you're asking for all documents with both terms. If a page contains "Vermont" but not "catamount," you're indicating that you're not interested. If it contains "catamount" but not "Vermont," you're also not interested.

- **OR:** When you place OR between two specified terms, you're indicating that you want records containing *either* of those keywords. By so doing, you're expanding your search parameters.

   Search example: money OR dough OR "legal tender"

   This means that you're interested in documents with any or all of these search terms.

   In this example, the quotation marks around "legal tender" indicate that you're interested in pages containing that precise phrase. "Legal" alone or "tender" alone is insufficient.

- **NOT:** When you place NOT in your search string, you're indicating that you *don't* want records containing the word that follows NOT.

   Search example: "World Series" NOT Yankees

   This means that you're interested in documents about the World Series, but not those that mention the Yankees.

These are the essential concepts of Boolean searching; understanding them will help narrow your online and off-line computer searches. There are also advanced searching techniques that build on these fundamentals, so be certain to master them.

Muckraking 101
Lesson Three: The Paper Chase

Talk about luck: The reference librarian at the Schuyler Public Library sends a clipping from the local paper about Tim Overpeck's troubles with APHIS, the federal agency responsible for inspecting zoos. According to the article, Wildest Things Animal Park was cited for unspecified violations of the Animal Welfare Act and the park's operator agreed to pay a $1,000 fine.

A **call to APHIS's Maryland headquarters** yields a thee-year-old **press release** announcing the agency's action. But the document says only that the Agriculture Department and Wildest Things reached a consent decree—that the zoo neither admitted nor denied any violations of the Animal Welfare Act but agreed to the $1,000 civil penalty. APHIS inspectors, the release adds, found problems in the area of recordkeeping.

A copy of the Animal Welfare Act is dug out of the **government depository library** at a nearby university, but it doesn't offer much insight into what Overpeck's transgressions may have been. Another call to APHIS is largely unproductive: Information about the matter is available from the **case file**, an official says. Because the matter has been adjudicated by an administrative law judge, the file is available for inspection without requiring a Freedom of Information Act request.

But the file is located halfway across the country, so a **FOIA request** is immediately sent asking for copies of anything pertaining both to Wildest Things Animal Park and Tim Overpeck's animal-dealer operation. And then the search is expanded: **Similar requests are filed with the Department of Natural Resources in the two states** in which Overpeck does business.

That's just for starters, however. For example, the director of the Ebbinger Zoo said that Overpeck was involved with breeding programs designed to ensure the survival of endangered species. A quick search of a **newspaper index** reveals that the Interior Department has jurisdiction over these animals, so a **FOIA** request is sent for copies of any files related to Overpeck's activities.

At the same time, a **systematic literature search** is initiated. **Indexes of newspapers and magazines** are checked for stories about Overpeck and Wildest Things Animal Park. A **directory of special-interest magazines** turns up a list of animal-welfare publications; only one is available in the local library, so **calls are made to the other publications** asking for help tracking down stories. **Internet search engines** are used to look for references to Overpeck and Wildest Things, but none are found. So **requests for information are posted to online bulletin boards** that focus on animal-welfare issues.

A speedy reply arrives from the Interior Department: Tim Overpeck, it turns out, has no permit to breed, buy, and sell endangered species. That means either that he's doing it illegally or that Chuck Russo, the director of the Ebbinger Zoo, was lying about Overpeck's credentials.

Either way, something is fishy. The **investigation is now expanded** to include Russo and Ebbinger: Literature searches are redone, and FOIA requests are filed with the state Department of Natural Resources and APHIS. A **national zookeeper association is contacted** to learn whether Russo is a member, and **a national organization of zoos** is queried about the Ebbinger Zoo's accreditation. In addition, a FOIA request is sent to the **city manager** asking for the opportunity to inspect all of the Ebbinger Zoo's records of payments received for the past five years. The city manager calls to ask why the information is being requested. He's reminded that the state open-records law prohibits him from asking such questions, but he presses the issue. A letter arrives a few days later denying the request for this financial information. Instead, he says that all publicly available financial information is included in the zoo's annual report to the city, which may be inspected at the library.

A **civil-liberties group is contacted** to ask for advice on appealing the denial. In the meantime, a **search of court records** is undertaken. This includes federal, state, and municipal courts, but the indexes reveal nothing. Russo's **résumé,** which was included with the zoo's **annual report**, lists employment at two other facilities. The **court clerks** are contacted in those cities, and the second call turns up a five-year-old **divorce proceeding**. Arrangements are made to **view the file**, which requires a three-hour drive. But it's worth the gas money: In a **deposition**, Russo revealed that he earned money moonlighting for an animal dealer in Martinson named Timothy Overpeck.

Next: Going to the Source

CHAPTER FIVE

Giving Corporations the Business

When the Walt Disney Company decided to build a new theme park in Virginia, the Commonwealth's government rolled out the red carpet. It was a done deal — at least until some disgruntled citizens decided to pull up the welcome mat.

It is by now a well-known story: In November 1993, the Walt Disney Company announces that it will build a $625 million theme park—and a related development—on 3,000 acres of Virginia countryside, just miles from the site of the Civil War's two bloody Battles of Manassas (also known as Bull Run). "Disney's America," which has the enthusiastic backing of newly elected Virginia Governor George Allen, is conceived as a historical tour of the nation, with such attractions as a Lewis and Clark raft ride, a train trip through the Industrial Revolution, and virtual-reality re-enactments of Civil War skirmishes. To be located 35 miles west of the nation's capital, the park's promise of thousands of jobs and millions in annual tax revenue prompts the Commonwealth's General Assembly to pledge millions for road and sewer improvements, tourism campaigns, and other project-related expenses. Disney Chairman Michael Eisner promises that the theme park will open in 1998. It is, by all accounts, a done deal.

But in short order, the giant entertainment firm is under fire from bands of zealous opponents. What starts as a local zoning battle quickly becomes an issue of national interest, even national importance. Environmentalists insist that the park not only will pollute the region's air and water, but also will damage the Shenandoah National Park. A coalition of well-known historians lines up against the project, claiming it will trivialize history. From one coast to another, columnists and editorial writers weigh in with their opposition. Cartoonists lampoon Disney. Sixteen out-of-state U.S. Representatives, one of whom dubs this a "national issue," introduce a congressional resolution urging the company to abandon the site in Virginia's Piedmont region and look elsewhere. Over nine months, some 12,000 articles mentioning the controversy appear in the nation's press—the equivalent of the reporting on AIDS during that same period.

And then, ten months after announcing its plans, Disney unexpectedly waves the white flag. Top corporate officials brief a stunned Governor Allen on the decision and issue a statement that says the company will try to build an American-history theme park elsewhere—possibly even at another Virginia location. Opponents of the park celebrate. Pundits assess the political ramifications of the defeat. Another wave of editorials—universally hailing the outcome—appear in papers across the country. Days later, this battle is also one for the history books. End of story.

But for those fighting similar wars, the lessons of this campaign should never be lost. After all, other grassroots organizations wage the same sort of battles against would-be theme-park builders, and the world at large has no interest in—or even knowledge of—the struggle. How the entire nation came to raise a collective voice against this particular project was hardly through happenstance. It was the result of a well-crafted strategy—one that other Goliath-slaying muckrakers can learn much from.

The urban sprawl that reaches beyond the Washington Beltway has not yet encroached heavily on the section of Prince William County that's home to the Manassas National Battlefield Park, where Confederate soldiers twice defeated their Union counterparts. Much of Loudoun County, to the north and east, is also still pristine, while Fauquier County, due south and west, is horse country, known for its grassy pastures, country roads, and magnificent estates. This area is also known around Washington, D.C., for its high-profile residents, whose likes include well-to-do (and well-connected) businesspeople, writers, politicians, and other luminaries.

The idea that 30,000 visitors a day would soon invade their tranquility spurred these residents to immediate action. Just hours after Disney announced its plans, the Piedmont Environmental Council, which for two decades had fought to keep development in check, hired attorney Chris Miller to coordinate an anti-theme-park campaign. Miller was trained in environmental law and policy, and had a background in other land-use-related issues that would be key to this struggle. He also had confidence that despite the opponent's deep pockets and political backing, this struggle was winnable.

"The bottom line is that the law was on our side," he says. "Disney had serious procedures to go through. The feeling was that the park was a good idea in a horrible place."

Disney's strategy, he adds, was easy to predict: Certain provisions in the law gave the company only nine months to win approval of the deal. "And we knew we had to slow them down," says Miller, who today is PEC's director.

Slowing down the Disney juggernaut proved to be a laborious task that required a staggering $2.5 million budget. Hundreds of area residents volunteered their time, money, and expertise, and the anti-theme-park staff grew to a full-time equivalent of 25. Lawsuits were filed to head off construction. Virginia legislators, who early on expressed near-unanimous support for the project, were lobbied to study the matter more closely before deciding whether to allocate funds to it. It was, says Miller, a frustrating process, because the incremental gains made in winning over support were not immediately apparent to worried theme-park detractors. But a three-month lobbying effort produced some key legislative victories that signaled a shift in momentum—a message to Disney that it couldn't win this game in a walk.

Freedom of Information Act requests were filed not only with Virginia, but also with federal agencies and every state in which Disney had built a theme park or had proposed to do so. The blanket strategy, says Miller, proved effective for a variety of reasons. For example, the same question asked of three different agencies yielded entirely different documents. Moreover, documents released by federal agencies produced revelations that Virginia had tried to keep secret. "We then asked the state, and they'd deny it," says Miller. "The number of times public officials would lie was amazing, and we could hold them accountable."

The fight for documents was ongoing, and the state's refusal to release some files resulted in court action. In one instance, a judge sided with PEC and instructed the state to list all the documents being withheld and the reason for the secrecy. The release of this list provided fresh clues to what types of information the state was guarding—revelations that helped PEC plan other parts of its campaign. In some instances, the state inadvertently turned over damaging information that legally could have been withheld. Collectively, says Miller, these documents demonstrated that officials weren't protecting the interest of Virginia. They showed, for instance, that analyses had not been performed to test Disney's assertions about the project; instead, lawmakers simply accepted Disney's premises unchallenged. Knowing this information gave theme-park opponents valuable insight into crafting their strategy.

That strategy also included a massive public-relations effort. And this is what really distinguished the fight.

It started with an immediate "scream of pain"—a print and radio blitz to lay out key issues for the community. That scream needed to be a loud one, because polls showed that 90 percent of Northern Virginia residents approved of the theme park. The 75 groups that banded together as an informal anti-Disney coalition had their work cut out for them.

There were internal debates about how best to approach the PR strategy. Some wanted to make it a single-issue campaign and to keep hammering at that one issue, but the idea was ultimately tabled. "We said, 'We have to have a hundred things in play, and different things will stick,'" says Miller. "Disney could never anticipate what would hit them next."

One component of that strategy was to patiently court the media, which jumped on the Disney bandwagon and rarely questioned the statements of company officials. "It took three months of hard work to get the press to understand that we were credible," says Miller. "We spent a lot of time talking to reporters to get them to understand details."

The accuracy and relevance of the anti-Disney materials helped both to frame the other side of the debate and, at the same time, to assure reporters that they could trust their opposition sources. Eventually, in fact, journalists to whom Disney pitched story ideas in turn consulted PEC for help with their reporting.

But the gambit that really scored a direct hit on an unprepared Disney was the group's attention to local history. This stretch of Virginia is home to the nation's most important collection of Colonial, Revolutionary, and Civil War sites. There are thirteen historic towns and another seventeen historic districts within an hour's drive. A two- or three-hour drive can take you to Thomas Jefferson's Monticello, or to Jamestown, the place where English settlement began. George Washington once surveyed some of this land.

To Disney, those were merely historical footnotes. But to the residents plotting ways to squelch the proposed theme park, those sites would be used as rallying points. After all, Disney officials may not have cared much about the Civil War, but many Americans did. The theme park, as Miller says, would be trespassing on history.

Instead of pushing that notion itself, the group turned to well-known historians such as Harry Truman biographer David McCullough, Pulitzer Prize-winning author James McPherson, and popular historian Shelby Foote, who rose to prominence in Ken Burns's public-television series on the Civil War. Burns, who was under contract to Disney, also chimed in against the project.

The two dozen historians, who called their group Protect Historic America, insisted that this was not the site for such a project. The area surrounding the battlefields would be littered with development, they argued, and a vital piece of America's heritage would be forever scarred. When Virginia leaders portrayed the groups as outsiders butting in on the Commonwealth's business, Foote had a ready reply: "Nobody's an outsider at Manassas or in the Shenandoah Valley. That belongs to all people."

By focusing on the historical significance of the region, the fight was successfully recast as a battle of national importance. Suddenly, chief executive officers of Fortune 500 companies were aligned with environmentalists. Conservative and liberal newspaper columnists were writing much the same words. Disney was simply outflanked.

It was, in fact, an issue that bedeviled the entertainment company. PEC was blessed with an impressive pool of local talent, including a marketing veteran who had crafted some of the nation's most memorable campaigns. This one also resonated with the public.

As a result, the media steamroller began bearing down on Disney: In paper after paper, the editorials criticized the company for daring to cheapen one of America's most sacred shrines. And closer to home, public opinion also started to shift: By the time Disney threw in the towel, polls showed that three-quarters of Northern Virginia residents opposed the project. And if Disney officials thought they could survive this onslaught, there was another matter to consider: It was subtly communicated to them that a shareholder lawsuit may be in the offing—litigation that would open them up to internal scrutiny about the advisability of this project. With Wall Street to consider, the stakes got higher.

Chris Miller says there are a number of lessons to be learned from this experience, but two stand out. The first is simply: You may lose every battle and still win the fight; perseverance, he says, is key. Second: Look to utilizing the talents of the community. Miller admits that his area is blessed with some renowned residents, but he believes that the skills to wage a good fight are everywhere.

"The talent pool in your community," he says, "is probably bigger than you think."

Tricks of the Trade

There is no precise formula for investigating the affairs of a corporation. Instead, the search for corporate information is typically a series of logical steps that, in turn, require you to use your intuition about where to look next. There are, however, some basic, big-picture strategies that will help lay the groundwork for virtually any investigation. Consider the advice of veteran reporter Larry Gurwin, coauthor of

False Profits, which chronicles the scandal involving the Bank of Credit and Commerce International:

> If the company is in a regulated industry, there might be a lot of information available from government agencies. If it has a liquor license, for example, you can often get detailed information on answers from license applications required by the local liquor control board. If you're investigating a broadcaster, you can get information from the Federal Communications Commission. If it's a bank, you can get information from banking regulators. If there has been litigation against the company, background information on its owners, officers, and so on might be available in court papers. In particular, look for depositions of key officers, since they're often asked for detailed summaries of their careers or background.
>
> All U.S. companies are incorporated in a particular state, and the agency where incorporation papers are filed—usually called the Secretary of State—is located in the state capital. You can get the Secretary of State's files, although the amount of disclosure varies considerably from state to state. It's also possible to get Dunn & Bradstreet reports, although they can be very expensive and the information may not always be reliable. You can also look in corporate directories, many of which are available in public libraries. There may also have been profiles of the firm in trade and industry publications, as well as the local press in the jurisdiction in which the company is located.
>
> If you want to do more detective work, you can talk to former employees, competitors, and suppliers. If the company is unionized, the trade unions may have a lot of information to share. But the best information is often available from adversaries, including people who have sued the company.

Corporate Scrutiny

Sometimes it takes a Herculean effort to ferret out revealing information about a company. Other times, however, the company has no choice but to hand over the goods.

Investigating privately held firms is generally more difficult than scrutinizing public corporations, because federal law requires the latter to file reams of information. But don't assume that the absence of such responsibilities gives private companies an impenetrable wall to hide behind. In addition to the articles of incorporation and annual reports required by the Secretary of State, the company may be required to file forms with a state department of labor, a worker's-compensation board, or another agency. In addition, check municipal and county records for such things as business licenses, occupancy permits, deeds, liens, and mortgages. Local and district courts may also hold answers. Company officials may make speeches, and employees may deliver technical papers that reveal something about the firm's inner workings. If the company offers plant tours to the community, those offer another opportunity to gather data.

If a company is publicly held, documents filed with the Securities and Exchange Commission may go a long way toward answering your questions. Among the key documents that may prove helpful:

- **Annual report.** This is the place to start, because an annual report lays out everything from corporate history to management, subsidiaries, and product reviews.

- **Form 10-K.** A comprehensive annual report of financial information, including descriptions of properties owned and the backgrounds of officers and directors.

- **Proxy statement.** This formal notice of matters to be voted on at shareholder meetings discloses information not found in other records.

- **Form 8-K.** This details recent changes that are of importance to shareholders or federal regulators, including corporate takeovers and resignations of directors.

- **Form 10-Q.** An unaudited quarterly financial statement.

The SEC also receives a wide array of forms from those companies going private, offering the sale of new securities, fighting "hostile" takeovers, and the like. These documents may be viewed at the SEC's Public Reference Room in Washington, D.C. Copies of 8-K and 10-Q forms are also available at the SEC offices in Chicago and New York City.

If these offices aren't within easy reach, try the Electronic Data Gathering, Analysis, and Retrieval system, or EDGAR, which makes some—but not all—of a company's SEC filings available online at no cost. The EDGAR home page is easy to navigate, and its search engine will find all available company documents since 1996. The Web site is www.sec.gov/edgarhp.htm.

Nonprofit Examinations

Nonprofit organizations may be exempt from paying federal tax, but they're not exempt from filing forms that permit outsiders to peek in on the operation.

When investigating a nonprofit, the place to start is with the Internal Revenue Service. To be granted nonprofit status, an organization must file IRS Form 1023. This form provides such information as names, addresses, and compensation of officers and directors; gifts, grants, and contributions received; income from unrelated business activities; corporate stocks and bonds; and other tidbits that will give you insight into the organization. By law, an organization's Form 1023 must be available for inspection at its offices during business hours. If you want to keep your inquiries confidential, however, copies of the application are available from the IRS district in the state where the group was founded. And if you're uncertain whether an organization is in fact legally tax-exempt, consult IRS Publication 78, *Cumulative List of Organizations*. Or search the database of tax-exempt groups on the IRS Web site, **www.irs.ustreas.gov/prod/bus_info/eo/eosearch.html**.

In addition to Form 1023, Form 990 (or Form 990-PF for a private foundation) will help you piece together information about a nonprofit. Filed annually, this form chronicles everything from assets and liabilities to contributors, political activities, and financial ties between the foundation and its managers.

Bear in mind that scrutiny of Form 990 should be just one component of a broader investigation. If the form reveals, for example, that the nonprofit has a for-profit subsidiary, initiate a methodical search of that entity using directories, newspaper databases, documents filed with the secretary of state, and so on. Check court records, leases, land records, and anything else that may be pertinent.

Form 990 is also available for inspection at an organization's office or at the appropriate IRS regional office.

One of the best sources for information about nonprofits is the Foundation Center, which maintains complete, publicly accessible collections at its office in New York City and its field office in Washington, D.C. More limited materials are available at the center's regional-collection offices in Atlanta, Cleveland, and San Francisco, as well as at more than 200 cooperating collections across the nation. To check on locations or holdings, call (800) 424-9836, or visit the center's Web site at www.fdncenter.org.

Mining Annual Reports

Here's a president's message you'll never read in an annual report: "I'm sorry to report that our company had truly disastrous results last year, and you can bet on more of the same over the next twelve months. In fact, only a fool would own shares of this sinking ship."

Annual reports provide a good window on a publicly held corporation, but even for those firms on a collision course with ruin, the glass typically has a rose-colored tint. And it's no wonder: These documents are crafted to generate enthusiasm for the company's stock. They're intended as a sales vehicle for individual and, increasingly, institutional investors. They're designed to convince current and would-be shareholders that management's ability to run a tight ship will add value to the share price over the coming year.

As a result, corporate highlights are loudly trumpeted, while debacles are couched in sugar-coated euphemisms like "unique challenge." It's no wonder, then, that an analysis of annual reports conducted not long ago by *Chief Executive* magazine showed honesty slipping to an all-time low: Nearly 15 percent of CEO letters to shareholders, the survey found, could not be deemed trustworthy. And a survey by Annual Reports, Inc., revealed that more than one-third of U.S. companies did not plan to mention current and potential environmental liabilities in their annual reports, as required by the Securities and Exchange Commission.

Nevertheless, more than half of the nation's institutional investors rank the annual report as the single most useful source of financial information. The chief executive officer and chief financial officer may be able to answer analysts' queries, and newspaper databases may produce dozens of stories, but it is the annual report, these key investors believe, that offers the greatest insight into a company.

For muckrakers, however, an annual report will rarely be the Holy Grail. The reason is simple: Savvy investors deconstruct an annual report's numbers in hopes of learning the true picture of a company's profitability (or lack thereof). This document may prove interesting, but it's not likely to produce the smoking gun that will turn your investigation around.

That's not to say that an annual report isn't useful. It can be of enormous value, because it will lay out both key facts about the company and dozens of potentially important leads. As a result, an annual report should always be included in the list of documents to scrutinize.

Obtaining such a report is as easy as requesting one from the company's office of shareholder relations. If you suspect that your investigation may be a long-term campaign, buy a single share of stock. Your share price, plus brokerage commission, will bring you an annual report, proxy statements, and an invitation to the annual meeting. As an interested shareholder, you may also be entitled to factory tours and other benefits that could prove useful to your work. Try to get a company's house organ, for example, as it may reveal more about a company's inner workings than any news article. It may include the names of suppliers or joint-venture partners—both rife with potential sources. These in-house publications also typically include key personnel changes, and someone leaving the firm could prove to be a valuable source.

Deciphering an annual report's financial information can be tricky. One of the best primers, *How to Read a Financial Report*, is available from the brokerage firm Merrill Lynch, including on their Web site, at www.ml.com/extpdfs/frhowtor.pdf. If you really want to delve into numbers, try Howard Schilit's book *Financial Shenanigans: How to Detect Accounting Gimmicks and Fraud in Financial Reports* (McGraw Hill, 1993). Information about the book, along with examples of corporate financial tricks the author uncovered, is available on the Web site of Schilit's Center for Financial Research & Analysis, www.schilit.com.

Deciphering an annual report's non-financials requires no additional study. Here are the key items in the document particularly worthy of your attention:

- **Subsidiaries, brands, and addresses.** The activities of related entities will no doubt give you important insight into the company's activities. Such knowledge will also let you logically expand your investigation to other states, where you can request copies of permits, troll for lawsuits, and so on. For example, the other states' air- and water-quality offices may have records on file about the company's operations. Similarly, an attorney general's office can tell you about environmental or other investigations.

- **Discontinued operations.** If the parent company sold a subsidiary, key personnel of that former property could prove to be important sources.

- **Officers and directors.** Do their affiliations and past activities shed light on the nature of your investigation? Have they been involved in lawsuits that may be pertinent? A comparison of the names from year to year may reveal ousted personnel who have gripes to air.

- **Competition.** Some reports include an analysis of the competition. Sources at those companies could prove helpful.

- **Footnotes.** Reserve the magnifying glass for this section of the report; it's where you'll learn about pending litigation and other critical matters. For example, a Virginia company explained in a footnote that a subsidiary was a defendant in a class-action suit that alleged exposure to chemicals and property devaluation resulting from previously conducted wood-treating operations: "The Company is also involved in proceedings with respect to environmental matters including sites where the Company has been identified as a potentially responsible party under federal and state environmental laws and regulations." It may be a routine footnote admission, but it certainly provides clues about the likely existence of potentially valuable court documents and regulatory-agency documents.

Be aware that public companies aren't the only entities that publish annual reports. Many government agencies, nonprofit organizations, and private groups also produce them. But the annual reports that states require of corporations (all but four states mandate that they be filed) are entirely different documents. They're not intended to entice investors; rather, they merely lay out such information as the company's address, names of officers, state of incorporation, and so on. Each state requires different corporations to file different information. One of the best reference works for determining state-by-state filing data and other means of unearthing corporate background is *How to Find Information About Companies*, published by Washington Researchers, Ltd. This three-volume set on company research and competitive intelligence will help you piece together just about any company's story. Information about the books, which carry *very* steep price tags, is available from the publisher at P.O. Box 19005, Washington, D.C. 20036-9005; (202) 333-3499. Or visit the company's Web site at www.researchers.com.

Muckraking 101
Lesson Four: Going to the Source

To recap: A keeper at the Ebbinger Zoo claimed that surplus animals were being handed over to a suspicious person, but when questioned, zoo director Chuck Russo insisted that the recipient—Tim Overpeck—was a respected animal dealer, only a handful of animals were involved in the transactions, and this inquiry was therefore unwarranted. When the town's mayor sided with Russo and praised him for his work, the citizens' advisory board that monitors zoo activity dropped the matter. However, a leery board member's subsequent investigation of federal, state, and local records revealed that Overpeck also owned an out-of-state animal park that had been fined for violations of animal-welfare laws. Furthermore, divorce records showed that zoo director Russo had once been employed by Overpeck.

Call it coincidence. Or an apparent conflict of interest that warrants further scrutiny.

Even a greenhorn muckraker should know that something stinks in the town of Ebbinger, and it ain't just the elephant yard on an August afternoon. Many of the mysteries could undoubtedly be cleared up by examining the municipal zoo's records, which were requested under the state's Freedom of Information Act. But the city manager still refuses to release the documents, and a lawsuit to force disclosure could be time-consuming. Instead, other avenues are pursued.

The **whistleblowing zookeeper is contacted for an off-the-record interview**. The call is placed to her home so she's free to speak without concern, and she's reminded to not speak on a cordless phone—a precaution against being overheard by a neighborhood hobbyist with a police scanner. This **confidential source** has valuable information, such as how many animals have left the zoo over the last few years, their names, their ages, and so forth. The information is added to a **computer database** that permits it to be easily retrieved. She also offers to conduct an after-hours theft of records from the director's office, but the offer is categorically refused. A decision was made early on to keep the investigation lawful, and the **state press association** was contacted for guidelines on the legality of tape-recording phone conversations, combing through someone's garbage, and other potentially questionable activities.

How many of these departing animals ended up with Tim Overpeck is the key question. The **contact at the Department of Natural Resources** suggests calling the **state Department of Agriculture,** which has responsibility over the interstate movement of animals. A clerk there says that a zoo animal moving to another state is usually accompanied by a so-called health certificate, copies of which are kept by the department's Division of Animal Industries. A **FOIA is filed** to inspect the records, but only a single certificate is found from the Ebbinger Zoo—paperwork for a kangaroo that was shipped to an out-of-state veterinary clinic. The informant zookeeper claimed that dozens of animals leave the zoo each year, so their disposition remains a mystery.

Books in Print is consulted for authors with zoo expertise. Three names surface. **Newspaper indexes are searched for book reviews**, which are called up on **library microfilm**. One author is identified as a university professor, and a **call to the school's switchboard** yields his office phone number. The mystery is explained, and in a **phone interview** he offers an explanation: These health certificates are required only when animals are moved across state lines; they're not required for intrastate transactions, so perhaps the Ebbinger Zoo's animals are all remaining in state. Maybe, he goes on to speculate, they're ending up with this guy Overpeck.

Another call is made to the **Division of Animal Industries** to arrange a **follow-up inspection of records**. The director expresses annoyance about the request, noting that files will have to be pulled again from a back room. But he's reminded that the state law does not limit citizens to a single search, and the request is faxed to his office. The second time is a charm. **Overpeck's file** contains a stack of documents showing that he moved zoo animals to auction houses in other states. What's more, many of the certificates include **names, ages, tattoos, and other data** that identify them as the animals in the database. The zoo director's contention that Overpeck received only two or three animals obviously isn't true. Overpeck has actually sold dozens of the Ebbinger Zoo's animals.

But why the lie? What sort of arrangement do these two have?

Next: Putting the Pieces Together

Chapter Six

Environmental Forces

*When the water in a Kentucky mobile-home park was found to be
contaminated, residents were assured that the potential health
consequences were inconsequential. But Joan Robinett didn't buy
that story, and she waged a search for truth that's a model for others facing the fallout of environmental mishaps.*

As birthdays go, Joan Robinett's 37th wasn't exactly one for
the highlight reel.

In fact, she celebrated the event in an Atlanta file room, some
300 miles from her home in Kentucky coal-mining country. In the
days before this less-than-memorable anniversary, Robinett had bat-
tled the Environmental Protection Agency for access to information
about her community's drinking water—an endlessly frustrating
process she now likens to pulling teeth. So when the invitation to
review the pertinent materials was finally extended, Robinett headed
for the Georgia capital.

This late-December road trip held great promise, because the EPA
apparently had stacks of data related to the cleanup of water contamination in Dayhoit, Kentucky. The residents of this tiny
Appalachian town, tucked away in the southeastern corner of the
state, had for years sought details about the consequences of drinking
the chemical-laden well water that once flowed from their faucets.
Robinett had led the fight for answers after state officials conducting

routine tests declared the water in the town's mobile-home park unsafe to drink and, as a short-term remedy, trucked in bottled water. Robinett had moved away from Dayhoit's Holiday Mobile Home Park just prior to the revelations, but she nonetheless feared that long-term exposure threatened her family's health.

"You spend 40, 60, 80 hours a week—you live it, you breathe it, you eat it," Robinett says of the campaign for information she hatched on the heels of this unnerving discovery. "When these disasters happen, it becomes—and it is—a matter of survival."

The loss of water was at first deemed more of an inconvenience than a cause for alarm. And a month later, at a town meeting convened by state and federal officials, residents were by and large satisfied with explanations of the situation. The source of the contamination, it was revealed, was a nearby industrial plant: Solvents used to clean and refurbish large machinery there had been dumped along the banks of the Cumberland River, and the chemicals had apparently leached into the groundwater. Residents of the mobile-home park were told that a dozen local wells had tested positive for at least four organic chemicals, and, to ensure their safety, a line would be run from their 70-home community to the city's water system, Don't drink the well water, they were told. Don't bathe in it, wash your cars with it, spray your lawns or gardens with it, and everything will be fine.

But then came the newspaper headline that followed a second town meeting: "Chances of Developing Cancer from Chemicals Found in Water Slim."

"That really caught my attention," says Robinett, "because at that point it hadn't really been emphasized that they were cancer-causing chemicals."

That revelation—that the tap water flowing to her former home had possibly been carcinogenic—sent Robinett off in search of the truth. It was at times a seemingly dead-end chase, as Robinett's queries were passed like relay batons from one expert to another. It was a quest that lasted years, and one that ultimately brought her to this Atlanta file room for yet another round of inquiry.

This time, a Freedom of Information Act request was supposed to yield stacks of raw data generated in developing reports for the EPA. "But when I got there," says Robinett, "I was presented with seven volumes of the administrative record, which is on file at my library. I said, 'Excuse me, but I can see this in Harlan County. I didn't drive all this way to Atlanta for this.'"

In fact, that's all the EPA staff made available to her that day. The reason: There was a "PRP"—a primarily responsible party—overseeing the cleanup of the contamination site, and the raw data was housed at this contractor's offices.

And where might those offices be? Robinett asked. They have offices all over the country, she was told.

It was hardly the birthday present the community activist had hoped for.

But this was about par for the trap-laden course traversed by Robinett and other members of the group she formed, Concerned Citizens Against Toxic Waste. It's an experience shared by many seeking data related to environmental mishaps, health-related matters, and similar issues. In northwest Arkansas, for instance, a citizens' group upset about a pipeline being routed through their neighborhood was forced to file a series of lawsuits after being denied documents under the state's Freedom of Information Act. When farmers in Wisconsin and Florida expressed concerns about the safety of a bovine growth hormone, the product's manufacturer withheld such information from regulatory agencies. A citizen finally sought "secret" information about the drug via a FOIA request, prompting three members of Congress to ask that the Food and Drug Administration address the controversy.

The difficulty of Robinett's task was magnified by the technical nature of the information she sought. Although state officials maintained that the risks of contracting cancer from the chemical-laden water were slim, Robinett wanted to verify those assurances. Her group's first stop was the local health department, but no one there had the required expertise. Robinett then tried universities—a time-consuming exercise that sent her phone bills soaring. One problem confronting her group was that members didn't really know what sort of information they wanted or needed; as a result, they asked university researchers for anything that might be available, generating a flood of seemingly useless information. But all of it was saved, a strategy that paid unexpected dividends: As their investigation unfolded and new issues were revealed, the archived material was sometimes found to be pertinent. The puzzle began to take shape.

Linking up with like-minded groups also helped advance Robinett's efforts. This process was set in motion by a phone call from an anonymous coal miner, who suggested contacting a longtime area activist. This contact in turn led Robinett to the director of a statewide environmental council, who put her in touch with a citizen's group in a neighboring county whose residents had waged a similar battle. The networking helped Robinett gain insight into the regulatory process, while also grounding her in specific issues related to water pollution.

Her organization's campaign proceeded simultaneously on a number of fronts. While the hunt for outside experts intensified, the group also interviewed current and former employees of the offending industrial plant about their health problems. These workers' firsthand knowledge, along with their stake in the community, made them particularly valuable assets. "They know what's going on inside the plant," says Robinett. "They know what the regulatory agencies are doing. They know what the company is or is not doing." For the first time, the citizens' group believed it could make connections between the workers' maladies and the unexplained symptoms—such as headaches and rashes—that often afflicted their children.

What's more, Concerned Citizens Against Toxic Waste initiated a campaign to wrest documents from state and federal agencies. The lesson learned in this phase of the campaign, says Robinett, was that the investigation of a company may lead you in numerous directions; as a result, tunnel vision can be counterproductive. Pay attention to the structure of the state government, she counsels, and also be aware of the federal-agency offices located in your state.

For example, the state health department may handle matters related to groundwater contamination, or a state environmental agency may have jurisdiction. If there is soil contamination, contacting a state waste-management program may be appropriate; if a landfill is the source of the problem, another agency may keep pertinent documents. Although Robinett's group found valuable information in EPA documents, a search of inspection reports generated by the Occupational Safety and Health Administration also proved revealing. In short, all avenues need to be explored.

This endless pursuit of facts sometimes made Robinett more knowledgeable than the so-called experts. While a site-assessment plan was being developed, for example, the Dayhoit citizens' group relied on plant workers to identify areas of environmental contamination. "We took state EPA people around the site and workers told them, 'I dumped waste material over here. We had burning over here. We had a little incinerator over here.' So we began to show them."

And research even helped Concerned Citizens Against Toxic Waste develop familiarity with specialized equipment like the airstripper, which the EPA had tabbed as a solution to one component of the Dayhoit problem. The group first learned of this device while poring through memoranda. Robinett has a friend who's an engineer, and when he told her of an Ohio company that manufactures the equipment, she called for brochures. "So they sent me this big color catalog of airstrippers and their different components, what they cost to operate, and what each did," Robinett recalls. "So by the time it came to going to the first meeting with the state EPA, we knew lots about airstrippers. We knew they didn't work. And we knew that what had been proposed for us was the cheapest made."

But Robinett's homework didn't stop there. She learned of a study that the EPA had conducted of 177 airstripping units—research that found the equipment to be largely ineffective. "So we went into this hearing, and they were pushing airstripping down our throats. And they asked, 'Why do you not want this piece of modern technology? What scares you about this?'

"I said, 'It's not the equipment; it's what you're saying it's going to do, and we know it's not going to do it. And we know it because your agency did a study of 177 of them.'

"And he said, 'I'm not familiar with that.'

"And I said, 'You're telling me you're an expert on airstripping?'"

Checkmate.

Or check, perhaps. Pressed by the group, the EPA agreed to bring in another airstripping expert. But the victory was Pyrrhic: This new expert was not an EPA employee. Instead, he had been hired by the company charged with cleaning up the pollution it had discharged in Dayhoit during the 1980s.

That struck Robinett and her peers as an obvious conflict of interest. But as they learned, in battles like this it's standard operating procedure.

They also learned that slugfests of this sort can go fifteen rounds, then begin all over. Dayhoit residents believe the evidence is unmistakable: Three and a half decades of pollution in their back yard, they say, has resulted in an unusually high cancer rate. But state environmental-protection officials maintain there is no hard evidence that the contamination caused any health problems. Furthermore, they say, there is no way to establish a cause-and-effect relationship between the specific industrial contamination and the Dayhoit community.

This impasse may never be resolved, but the cleanup goes on. The community group continues to monitor the issue, and Robinett's muckraking earned her a five-year gubernatorial appointment to Kentucky's Quality of Life Committee.

The struggle took its toll, however, putting a strain on her family life and alienating her from some in the community. Looking back, she advises others not to get overwhelmed by the amount of time it may take to accomplish their goals. "People should not let that stop them, not let that frustrate them to the point that they don't want to deal with it," she adds. "Because sooner or later, they'll get a hit. You just take it. Take it and run with it."

The Grand Tradition

So what exactly *is* a muckraker anyway?

Credit for popularizing the term goes to President Theodore Roosevelt, who was concerned about the zealous way in which turn-of-the-century journalists approached their work. Among the celebrated Progressive Era writers raising a voice against social injustice, dishonest government, and corrupt business practices were the likes of Ida May Tarbell, who crusaded in print against Standard Oil, and Lincoln Steffens, who enthusiastically tweaked politicians with such works as *Tweed Days in St. Louis*, a novel about municipal corruption. Perhaps the most famous of the crowd, however, was Upton Sinclair, whose novel *The Jungle* exposed the horrors of the Chicago meatpacking plants and spurred Congress to pass new laws.

President Roosevelt deemed such writers societal assets, "but only if they know when to stop raking the muck."

The work of these "muckrakers," who delved into everything from slum life to sweatshops, resembled that of investigative reporters. But there are differences between the two. In fact, as Harry H. Stein and John M. Harrison write in their book *Muckraking: Past, Present and Future* (Penn State University Press, 1973), the differences are significant.

"Investigative journalism encompasses the 'watchdog' function of the American press: the surveillance of governmental and political institutions and personnel and their conformance to ordinances and regulations and to social values and norms resembling law. Muckrakers exercise a surveillance over a wider area than government and politics and so have probed the unique and the common in American society, the highest reaches of power and the everyday social patterns of the population. Also, muckrakers sometimes define as a removable evil a practice or view normally accepted as natural, inescapable, or beneficent."

Similarly, the authors write, muckraking may also resemble advocacy journalism, in that it can make emotional appeals and personalize complex issues. But here, too, there are differences.

"Distinct from advocacy journalists, muckrakers have tried to preserve their autonomy, never irretrievably committing themselves to any single cause or person. They have checked their partisanship (but not their critical sensibilities) with a healthy skepticism, journalistic norms or instructions, and audience predilections."

So if your allies or adversaries deem your work worthy of a real muckraker, be aware that it's a label worthy of distinction.

Enviro-CAR

Computer-assisted reporting, or CAR, has been a godsend for anyone doing environmental muckraking. Virtually every major environmental organization has a Web site, making it easy to track down both information and sources. The Environmental Protection Agency has an extremely useful site (www.epa.gov), as do most of its state counterparts. In addition, there are numerous environmental newsletters, magazines, and news services online, many of which offer full-text searches of their archives.

In fact, the biggest stumbling block to conducting effective environmental CAR may be the sheer number of online opportunities. Fortunately, there are a few sites that serve as good jumping-off points to Internet-accessible materials, providing cataloged links to hundreds of useful home pages. Here are five good ones:

- **EnviroWeb** is a project of the nonprofit EnviroLink, which unites hundreds of organizations and volunteers around the world. The site provides links to a wide variety of environmental resources. Address: www.envirolink.org.

- **World Wide Web Virtual Library: Environment.** Maintained by the University of Virginia, this site offers a convenient way to search for organizations and agencies with expertise in specific issues and subjects. Address: earthsystems.org/Environment.shtml.

- **Galaxy** is a browsable/searchable Web directory with a broad range of indexed categories, including academic organizations, directories, government organizations, nonprofit groups, and periodicals. Address: galaxy.einet.net/galaxy/Community/Environment.html.

- **The Amazing Environmental Organization Web Directory** bills itself as the planet's biggest environmental search engine. Given its mind-boggling number of hyperlinks to organizations, there's probably no point in disputing the claim. Address: www.webdirectory.com.

- **The Society of Environmental Journalists** claims a membership of more than 1,100, most of whom are working journalists. SEJ's Web site, maintained in concert with the International Federation of Environmental Journalists, is a great one-stop source of environmental reporting tips and resources. In addition to a comprehensive collection of hyperlinks that is particularly strong on databases and government agencies, the home page also includes back issues of the organization's quarterly, *SEJournal*.

Glean some tips from journalists who cover environmental issues for a living. Of particular use is a regular "Online Bits & Bytes" column, which focuses on computer-assisted reporting techniques and opportunities. Address: www.sej.org.

Tips from "beat" reporters will invariably prove useful, since they've likely figured out shortcuts to unearthing the sort of information you may be after. What's more, they can probably lead you to databases you didn't know existed.

Here, for example, is a noteworthy tip from veteran environmental reporter Marianne Lavelle, coauthor, with Dan Fagin and the Center for Public Integrity, of *Toxic Deception: How the Chemical Industry Manipulates Science, Bends the Law, and Threatens Your Health* (Birch Lane Press, 1997):

> One of the best resources to begin searching for information on environmental problems is the Right-to-Know Network. It is a project of the public-interest group OMB Watch and the Unison Institute, a center for computer systems in the public interest. Both are based in Washington, D.C.
>
> In 1992, my colleagues and I at *The National Law Journal* produced "Unequal Protection," a special report on pollution in minority neighborhoods. At the time, we had to pay hundreds of dollars for government databases of fines against polluters and progress at Superfund toxic-waste cleanup sites. Then we had to pay $2,000 for U.S. Census data on the racial and economic breakdowns of the neighborhoods (by zip code). We found that fines against polluters were higher, and cleanup of toxic waste sites was faster, in white communities than in minority neighborhoods. All of the information we used to make those comparisons is now available online, for free, through RTKNET (www.rtk.net).
>
> You can search whether companies in your hometown (or any geographic region) have been fined by the federal government for violating laws. You can check out a particular corporation's record of violations and fines. You can obtain basic information on the location of Superfund sites and the pollutants present. Through the 'Records of Decision' database, you can also see what plans, if any, the federal government has made for cleanup of sites. You can check out the 'legal' releases of toxic chemicals in your neighborhood through the Toxic Release Inventory. You can look up health facts

about chemicals. You can ascertain the U.S. Census' racial and economic statistics for any region.

RTKNET also offers a host of databases that are not environmental at all. They include information on the fair-lending, fair-housing, and community-reinvestment practices of banks. This data is crucial for minority communities that are trying to learn if lenders are avoiding providing services to their neighborhoods—a practice known as "redlining."

To establish a free account, visit the RTKNET Web site. For additional information, call OMB Watch at (202) 234-8494 or the Unison Institute at (202) 797-7200.

Raising Your IRE

The best one-stop source of muckraking information is Investigative Reporters and Editors, a Missouri-based nonprofit organization founded in 1975. IRE helps train its members in the techniques of investigative reporting, focusing on everything from computer-assisted reporting to unearthing documents pertaining to cults, colleges, and financial discrimination.

Unfortunately, much of IRE's materials—most notably, the handouts from its conferences and seminars—are available only to members. But the organization publishes a number of valuable books also available to nonmembers. These include:

- *The Reporter's Handbook: An Investigator's Guide to Documents and Techniques, 3rd Edition.* If you want one overall compendium on ways to track down information in the private and government sectors, this is it. The *Handbook* is short on theory and heavy on practical, nuts-and-bolts techniques for getting the lowdown on individuals, politicians, corporations, and just about anyone (or anything) else. It tells you what's available and how to get it. Investigative reporters' war stories are included throughout, providing insight into techniques that proved effective for them. Cost: $30.

- *Investigative Environmental Reporting.* This handbook highlights successful environmental reporting, augmented by explanations of the techniques used. The book also includes a wide range of tips for environmental reporters, ranging from finding one's way around the Environmental Protection Agency to using data from the Toxic Release Inventory. Cost: $7.

- **How to Investigate Your Friends and Enemies.** Published in 1992, Louis Rose's 137-page book is a great primer on finding and using various public records, including property records, driver's licenses, and assessment taxes. Cost: $15.

These and other IRE publications may be ordered directly from the organization. For details and an order form, contact IRE at 138 Neff Annex, Missouri School of Journalism, Columbia, MO 65211; (573) 882-2042. IRE's Web site (www.ire.org) also includes book information.

The site offers other items of interest as well. For example, the "Training" portion of the site includes some details about the conference handouts—the ones available only to members. But the site also includes a state-by-state membership directory, so perhaps you can find a familiar (and possibly sympathetic) name on the list.

If that doesn't work, there are other ways of unearthing items of possible interest. For example, one of the handouts—"Background a Candidate"—is a six-page summary that includes information on such areas as corporate research, nonprofit organizations, political research, and the Postal Information FOIA form. If that sounds interesting, take heart: The author is private investigator Larry Zilliox, Jr., author of *The Opposition Research Handbook: A Guide to Political Investigations*. These subjects—and much more—are included in Zilliox's book, which is available from Investigative Research Specialists, 1390 Chain Bridge Road, Suite 10, McLean, VA 22101. The cost is $20 plus $3 shipping.

Tapes are available of the seminars at which these materials were handed out. So you may not get the printed matter, but you'll get a good summary, along with broader discussion. These can be ordered on the IRE Web site (www.ire.org).

So when you're denied access to documents you know exist, simply do what IRE would recommend to its members: Find another way to get your hands on them.

Anti-SLAPP Happy

First, the good news: You've spent months doggedly investigating a local factory suspected of polluting a nearby stream and its tributaries, and the work appears to have paid off. You've wrested documents from the EPA, pored over studies conducted by state regulators, interviewed confidential sources, paid for the analysis of water samples, examined the company's campaign contributions to sympathetic politicians, and pieced together reams of paper from out-of-state lawsuits against the parent company that show a pattern of environmental abuse. As a result, you have every reason to believe that the health of your community may be at risk, and you circulate a petition demanding that local lawmakers convene hearings to address the potentially dangerous situation. Score one for the time-honored tradition of citizen muckraking.

Now the bad news: Your efforts have not gone unnoticed by the company in question, whose attorney writes to inform you that the petition's disparaging remarks are not being taken lightly within the boardroom. In conclusion, the lawyer writes, here's your ultimatum: Drop the petition drive or prepare for a face-off in court.

Your first reaction is disbelief. After all, the First Amendment guarantees both the right of free speech and the right to petition the government for redress of grievances. Does this company believe it can strip you of those fundamental protections? What's going on here?

You're about to be SLAPPed.

In other words, the company has threatened to file a strategic lawsuit against public participation, or a SLAPP. The term was coined by University of Denver professors George Pring and Penelope Canan to describe an escalating—and alarming—trend: civic activists routinely being sued by the targets of their discontent. Such actions have been filed against those whose "crimes" include everything from testifying at hearings to reporting violations of law and writing letters to the editor. The SLAPP shots have been fired in large numbers at those engaged in zoning and real-estate-development battles, as well as those who criticize public officials and employees. Environmentalists have been a particular target of

SLAPPers, whose multimillion-dollar requests for damages are often enough to frighten activists into submission.

Consider examples of what some have encountered:

- A Pennsylvania woman filed a complaint with the state Department of Environmental Resources after acidic water from a stripmining operation destroyed her house. The mining company hit back with a SLAPP suit.

- County officials in Georgia threatened libel suits against local citizens who had petitioned for their removal from office.

- A Tennessee company filed suit against an environmental organization, charging that it had been defamed by statements the group made in a booklet examining its operations.

- When California residents spoke out against a businessman's proposal to build an apartment complex in their neighborhood, the developer filed a lawsuit against the residents, seeking $27 million in damages.

- A Rhode Island woman wrote a letter to state regulators expressing her concern that a landfill might be contaminating local groundwater. For her troubles, she earned a lawsuit that dragged on for four years.

Given the high costs associated with such litigation, many citizen activists either throw in the towel or stay out of the ring entirely. That, of course, is exactly what their deep-pocketed opponents are after: It's an end-game strategy designed to squelch free speech, stifle citizen activism, and erect a barrier to participation in the democratic process.

And it's often effective. "The ripple effect of such suits in our society is enormous," wrote Justice Nicholas Colabella, of the trial-level New York Supreme Court for Westchester County, in a developer's lawsuit against the Nature Conservancy. "Persons who have been outspoken on issues of public importance targeted in such suits or who have witnessed such suits will often choose in the future to stay silent. Short of a gun to the head, a greater threat to the First Amendment can scarcely be imagined."

Fortunately, those activists who do stick it out usually win the court fight, because the overwhelming majority of these suits are dismissed. Unfortunately, that outcome typically takes years. In the interim, the legal tab keeps escalating and the issue that first motivated the activists may just languish on the back burner, discouraging some from going ahead with their muckraking. But Canan, who with Pring authored *SLAPPs: Getting Sued for Speaking Out* (Temple University Press, 1996), believes the greater risk is to not get involved.

As Canan notes, those getting SLAPPed are returning the favor with "SLAPP-back" suits. In one case, a hospital worker who was sued for libel after criticizing an infectious-waste disposal company about its incinerator operation won an $86.5 million jury verdict against the firm. In another case, a trio of farmers won an $11.1 million verdict against a large agribusiness company that had filed a libel suit against them. The farmers' crime: running an advertisement that urged voters to support a water project. By opposing the project, the ad claimed, the agribusiness firm stood to gain a monopoly in the cotton industry.

Legislators are also coming to activists' defense. About a dozen states, including California and New York, have enacted so-called anti-SLAPP laws. These laws not only make it easier for the targets of SLAPP suits to prevail in court, but they also may provide for the recovery of attorneys' fees and other awards.

So if you choose to go forth with a muckraking campaign, be aware that your mere participation may cause you anguish. But staying on the sidelines carries its own serious consequences.

"Regardless of a state's having anti-SLAPP legislation, we have the political high road fundamental to our democratic system of government," says Canan, who with Pring has been examining the phenomenon since the mid-1980s. "In fact, early SLAPPs won large malicious-prosecution awards against SLAPP filers prior to state legislation or widespread recognition of the phenomenon.

"I do appreciate that SLAPP targets of today benefit from the knowledge that they are not alone, that their right to influence government is sacrosanct even if threatened, and that a SLAPP actually indicates that citizens are in fact being effective—otherwise there wouldn't be a SLAPP.

"Nevertheless, I do not want to sound cavalier in pushing others to keep up the fight, since it is obvious to them—as well as in the hundreds of cases we have learned of—that the fight is not fun. Yet brave, caring people are our best hope against such tyranny. We are all beholden to them for keeping democracy strong."

Muckraking 101
Lesson Five: Putting the Pieces Together

So Timothy Overpeck has been getting large numbers of animals from the Ebbinger Zoo, which are being sold at out-of-state auctions. And zoo director Chuck Russo wants to keep the matter secret.

Russo admitted in his divorce papers that he had once worked for Overpeck, so maybe the two still have a business arrangement. One plausible theory: Russo is giving Overpeck the zoo's surplus animals—instead of selling them to other zoos—and in return Overpeck is giving Russo kickbacks.

A **blanket search for information** about the two is set in motion. **FOIAs** are filed with local and state **law-enforcement agencies**. Requests are made for their **driver's license information and motor-vehicle records**. **Uniform Commercial Code records** are examined. **Military records** are requested. **Voter registration records** are scrutinized.

The small pile of paper that has accompanied this investigation has grown into something resembling a mountain. Fortunately, a **filing and tracking system** was set up from the start, so finding names, dates, and other information is relatively simple.

But digesting all this data and unearthing something that links the two men are other matters altogether. The available documentation is enough to show that dozens of the Ebbinger Zoo's animals are going to Overpeck, but that probably isn't enough to generate media coverage. After all, Russo could tell reporters what he told the citizens' advisory board: that Overpeck bought the animals, and that the money this licensed animal dealer paid has been used to upgrade the zoo's facilities. More documentation is needed to make the case.

On a hunch, the **marriage certificates** of both men are requested from the county clerks' offices. Pay dirt: Russo is married to a woman named Sherry Fitz. The name is familiar, and for good reason: **Records from the Secretary of State** show that a Sherry Fitz is both the treasurer of Tim Overpeck's business and a partner.

It's all falling into place. But one question remains: Why is the town clerk stonewalling? Why won't he release the zoo's financial records?

As a top political appointee, the town clerk must file a **financial-disclosure** form. The form reveals no outside income, other than interest from a passbook savings account. The city attorney probably instructed him to not release the documents, so her financial-disclosure forms are also scrutinized. Nothing telling there, either.

Of course, the city attorney probably consulted with the mayor on this matter—the very person who on day one downplayed the animal sales and lent his unbridled support for the zoo director. His financial-disclosure forms are eyeballed, along with his **campaign-finance records**. Curiously, there's a lone contribution from out of state—a large check from the employees of the Wildest Things Animal Park, in Schuyler, which happens to be Tim Overpeck's other business.

It's a tidy little circle. The zoo director is apparently giving away animals to a company that's owned, in part, by his wife, and that firm (his former employer) is in turn profiting from the sale of those animals. What's more, that company has donated money to a politician who is now protecting those involved in this scheme.

Call it conflicts of interest. Call it unseemly. Call it abuse of power or the public trust. Call it what you want, but don't forget to **call the press**.

Next: Going Public

CHAPTER SEVEN

Consumer Protection

All Rosemary Shahan wanted was to get her ailing car back in one piece. But when the repair shop gave her the runaround, Shahan's muckraking put it on a one-way road to ruin. Her efforts also provided a model for other wronged consumers looking for a way into the driver's seat.

Call it a case of turning a lemon into lemon aid.

For Rosemary Shahan, it was really a matter of seeing that justice was served—that the California car-repair shop responsible for causing her undue inconvenience was held accountable for its misdeeds. In the process, Shahan helped lift the curtain on unscrupulous auto-industry practices and arm consumers with heavy artillery for their skirmishes with Motor City bigwigs.

When her Volkswagen Dasher was involved in a minor collision, Shahan entrusted the car to a dealer in a San Diego-area town called, appropriately enough, Lemon Grove. The staff at John Factor Volkswagen promised that the repairs would be completed in two to three weeks, but three months later many of the replacement parts hadn't even been ordered. What's more, Shahan's displeasure over such treatment earned her a threat rather than an apology: File a complaint against the dealer, she was told, and the shop's mechanics would install unsafe components in her ailing 1978 Dasher.

"I think what really impressed me with that experience," says Shahan, "was that the dealer seemed to feel that it didn't really have the responsibility to fulfill its normal obligations. I went to all the authorities and all the government agencies, and they were very sympathetic but basically said I was on my own. There wasn't anything they could do. So in the absence of anything official, I was forced by events to act. It was desperation. I was desperate for my car."

That desperation forced a sign-carrying Shahan onto the sidewalk in front of the VW dealer—a strategy that didn't go unnoticed by the owner's son, who promptly called police to have her arrested. But Shahan had investigated her rights beforehand and knew that her free-speech activities were legal. Still, a solo crusader carrying a barely readable placard looked more like a company-sponsored advertising gimmick than an effort at restitution. No wonder, then, that a month of parading earned Shahan little more than a sunburn and the enmity—even threats—of dealer employees: Her dismantled car remained impounded behind the dealer's fence. And when the repairs were finally completed, she got anything but satisfaction. Although the shop's manager had agreed to let Shahan's mechanic examine the car, the offer was mysteriously withdrawn. Back to the picket line went the car-less Shahan, who would soon win a restraining order that prohibited the auto shop's increasingly belligerent staff from impeding her picket.

"All this time people were coming up to me," she recalls. "And when you stand up like this, people feel like you're standing up for them. They were telling me their problem with the dealership, or even with other dealerships or other manufacturers. And there were some real horror stories of people who were sold grossly unsafe vehicles. People would buy a new vehicle that just didn't work, and they'd be stuck having to make the payments on a vehicle they couldn't use. And I did some research in the court records and found out this dealer had been sued a lot."

Rosemary Shahan, teacher-turned-activist, had learned the value of both confidential sources and ferreting out government documents. As a result, the inattentive car dealer would soon learn that its opponent was in the driver's seat.

Actually, Shahan had already made use of tipsters in her months-long quest for relief. Early on, when she had hoped to learn the dealer's thoughts about the picket out front, her answers came via sympathetic neighbors posing as car buyers. Some allies even test-drove cars before offhandedly asking about the woman with the placard. She's a drunk driver, they were told. She even killed some pedestrians, the dealer let on.

So Shahan knew from the start that her nemesis was no stickler for truth. Alerted to other consumers' problems, she marched off to the San Diego courthouse to examine everything from municipal- and superior-court records to small-claims court documents—evidence-gathering missions that, she hoped, might reveal more dealer lies. It was an exercise that later proved valuable: "One time, the dealer had agreed to negotiate," she says, "and he said I was the only customer they had ever had any problems with. By then, I knew he'd been sued over a dozen times recently, and I had a list of other people who had problems there."

As Shahan's crusade continued, however, her interests expanded beyond her own out-of-commission Dasher. This shift was spurred, in part, by a query she was increasingly getting from people: We know this dealer isn't reputable, but where can we find one that is?

Shahan assumed that the court records might offer some answers, but instead they provided her evidence that dealers and manufacturers were selling vehicles they knew to be unsafe; for example, some were unloading onto hapless consumers "chopped" cars—pieced-together halves of automobiles that had been damaged in wrecks. In one instance, a car that a dealer had sold for thousands of dollars was deemed by police unsafe to drive. In another, a father of two young children was seriously injured when the steering mechanism held together with bailing wire snapped. In yet another case, a motorist lost limbs when her car caught on fire after being rear-ended.

Shahan's scrutiny of the documents eventually turned up evidence that one of the nation's Big Three automakers could have prevented accident-related burn deaths by spending money on vehicle redesign. The car company paid a multimillion-dollar settlement fee, after which the court records were sealed. Shahan had stumbled on four incriminating internal documents prior to the seal order but hadn't had the foresight to make copies—a lesson she warns others to consider. But a phone call to the *Los Angeles Times* nonetheless resulted in a page-one story about the automaker's settlement.

Almost by chance, Rosemary Shahan's personal fight for auto-related justice had moved well beyond Lemon Grove.

It moved, in fact, to the California state capital after Shahan realized that people buying lemons had no recourse. On the advice of a friend, she contacted a state Assemblyman and asked him to carry a bill that would be called the Lemon Law.

Connecticut actually beat California to the punch after a legislator there read about the California bill in a newspaper column. But Shahan's home state wasn't far behind with its Lemon Law, and eventually 48 more states extended to auto buyers a beefed-up measure of consumer protection.

Shahan helped this cause along by turning her one-woman crusade into Motor Voters, a nonprofit organization devoted to auto-safety issues. By teaming up with other like-minded groups, Motor Voters has helped focus public attention on such things as the need for airbags and shortcomings in auto owners' manuals. Eventually, Shahan's fight moved from the California sidewalks to the halls of Congress, where her statements were regularly solicited for auto-related legislation.

One tool that Motor Voters has long used to inform its members, the media, and lawmakers is a newsletter. The information in it comes from a variety of sources, says Shahan. "Some of it is original research; some of it we get from other organizations like the Insurance Institute for Highway Safety. Their research organization, the Center for Auto Safety, has been a great resource, an ally. Looking at court records is still a way to find out, first, what is happening to the individual consumer, and also getting information on the company—the internal documents from the company—is a way to have access to what's going on within these companies. They have a public persona and a public position, and you get these internal documents and you see that, wait a minute, there's quite a difference."

Sometimes information comes from confidential sources. For example, the California Department of Motor Vehicles was going to very quietly charge Chrysler with reselling defective vehicles without the required disclosure. But someone at the state agency slipped Motor Voters a copy of the complaint, which the group then publicized widely. That move earned Shahan a dinner with Chrysler executives as well as a lesson in fighting a corporation: "You can exchange pleasantries with people, but you know they have an agenda. And of course, they were very angry. Instead of blaming themselves for being in this fix, they blamed me for exposing it."

So Rosemary Shahan became a prominent activist—an auto-industry watchdog who earned this assessment from Ralph Nader: "As tenacious as a bull, consistent as the Milky Way, and as humane in her own way as Mother Teresa." And her organization became national in scope.

But what ever became of her downed VW Dasher?

The dealer finally bought it from her—a proposal of hers that had at first been rejected outright. And the dealer paid her $25 per day from the time the repairs were supposed to have been completed until the settlement was reached. The car that was worth about $6,000 brought her a $10,000 check, not to mention a new career.

After that, the car dealer folded its tent. The space was later taken over by a pizza parlor. You'll see pedestrians milling about, but don't look for protesters.

Rules of Engagement

Some reporters treat the search for information as if it were a full-contact sport: If doing the job requires them to be rude, aggressive, or obnoxious, then so be it. Hey, investigative reporting isn't a popularity contest; it's a tedious search for answers. And as everyone knows, nice guys finish last.

That's indeed often the case: The pushy reporter gets the story, and the mild-mannered one returns to the office empty-handed. Sometimes, in fact, you have to be aggressive or you simply won't get satisfaction. But as others have learned, there are less confrontational ways to get the job done. Here are three valuable ones:

- Bureaucrats just don't get much respect. People demand documents or publications, and seem to react only when their request is not filled expeditiously. As a result, those who treat these workers with respect stand out from the crowd—a distinction that can help to cut through red tape when subsequent requests are filed. So when a government worker sends you the requested documents, reply with a thank-you note. That worker may be the keeper of other pertinent documents, and a little courtesy can go a long way next time around.

- A Pulitzer Prize-winning journalist who's a master of prying loose information has a favorite technique for getting hard-to-reach people on the phone: Be nice to secretaries. While others may disregard these workers, this journalist always tries to learn the name of a source's assistant, and then records it in his Rolodex. Secretaries, after all, are the buffer between outsiders and their bosses, and they can put one person's phone message at the top of the pile and relegate another's to the bottom, even the wastebasket. So when this journalist phones a hard-to-reach official, he calls the secretary by name and exchanges pleasantries. The often-overlooked assistant usually appreciates the recognition, which translates into access to the boss.

- There is a journalistic code of ethics that dictates when a source may be quoted by name, and, to the credit of reporters, breaches of the code are rare. Unfortunately, the rules are not only vague, but also different from city to city. In fact, reporters in the same town—or even at the same newspaper—will often disagree about how the game is played: Some will tell you that "deep background" means the information can never be used, while others believe that it can be used in print, but without being quoted directly and without attribution. To complicate matters, the sources themselves may have totally different ideas about how their requests for anonymity should be interpreted. So when someone being interviewed says, "This is off the record," she may mean that no direct quote should appear in print. The reporter, however, may take an off-the-record request to mean that the source's name should be omitted, but the material is fair game. He may therefore quote the person and attribute it to "a source" or "an official."

Muckrakers are often faced with the same dilemma. After all, their reporting may —indeed, should—one day be released in a report, used in an op-ed piece, or handed over to journalists. As a result, their sources need to feel comfortable that their trust won't be violated.

In general, most journalists—and the politicians and business leaders they often interview—take "off the record" to mean that the person may not be quoted but that the material may be summarized for use in a story. Some sources will ask to be interviewed "on background," which means that they may be quoted directly, although not by name.

It can be a confusing ritual, because you may hang up on a phone call without knowing for sure whether the person wants his name kept secret. The general rule to follow, then, is the one that reporters use with an unfamiliar source: If the conversation is deemed off the record, request a clarification. And if you don't like the ground rules, try to maneuver things to your advantage. For example, if a town-council member prohibits you from using her information in print, point out that it's therefore of no value. Ask if you can simply use the material without revealing where it came from.

Whatever agreement is reached, honor it. After all, using a city official's provocative quote may earn you media coverage, but consider the long-term consequences: When your group has another ax to grind, you'll likely find one less ally in the town hall.

The Inside Scoop

When WCAU-TV aired a six-part series on insurance-industry rip-offs in June 1997, the reporter blowing the whistle was Herb Denenberg. Who better than Denenberg to tip off Philadelphia-area viewers to an insurance-industry ploy that gives policyholders the shaft? After all, not only has Denenberg been the station's consumer and investigative reporter for 23 years, but consider some of his other credentials: He has served as Pennsylvania insurance commissioner, Pennsylvania public-utility commissioner, and a professor of insurance at the University of Pennsylvania's Wharton School. For good measure, he's a syndicated columnist, too.

Similarly, who better than Herb Denenberg to give citizen muckrakers some tips from the other side of the fence? He is often approached by citizens and organizations with stories of government ineptitude or corporate malfeasance; some succeed in their efforts to interest him, while others don't make the grade. Denenberg is known for his candor, and here's a telling sampling of it:

> The tobacco industry has been able to buy Congress and state legislatures over the decades, while killing 400,000 a year and lying about its holocaust-generating activities. If you sell out to the tobacco industry, you can sell out to anybody from the devil on up. Congress has long been sold out to tobacco. That carries good news and bad news.
>
> The bad news is that our system is relatively indifferent to right or wrong if enough political influence, raw power, or money is behind someone or something. The good news is that the system is also responsive to pressure from good organizations and good causes.
>
> But if you want to influence the system, you can't be lazy, faint of heart, lacking in guts, or without brains, planning, and organization. Anyone has a good chance to make significant changes in the system and correct problems and injustices; it's possible, in fact, to make huge changes. But it takes more than the proverbial eternal vigilance. It takes work and know-how properly applied. Sometimes you can get lucky and accomplish your objectives with little effort. But don't expect to be lucky every time.

Here are three of Denenberg's strategies for effectively approaching the media:

Rule One: Know the Media and Persevere

If you have a story to sell or a cause to promote, you've got to view it as a product and the media as your market.

The media is the market. That means you've got to know the media. You have to do more than read newspapers and magazines, watch TV, listen to the radio, and surf the Web. You have to know which reporters and media outlets might be interested in your cause or story ideas. Approach those that have demonstrated a receptiveness to your kind of story. For example, if you want to expose unnecessary surgery or incompetent dentistry, you can figure out which reporters are cheerleaders for the health-delivery system and which are interested in exposing wrongdoing and abuse of power. You can figure out which ones are shills for new drugs and surgical procedures and which ones are interested in stopping unnecessary surgery and medical malpractice.

You have to get to know the reporters, editors, producers, and others involved both in reporting stories and in deciding which are to be investigated. Get on the phone. Send them press releases and other background information. Let them know you're not going to fade away. Visit them. Stay on them. I've done many stories over the years that I would not have done but for the unbelievable perseverance of someone who wanted the story told. Don't underestimate the power of a persevering pest.

Remember that the media do little original work. Most of their creative energies go into ripping off stories from other media outlets. So don't just hit the biggest newspaper or television stations. Hit every kind of media outlet, even the smallest ones. You can then use that coverage as leverage to get a media outlet higher in the pecking order to pick up the story. Don't assume any outlet is too big or too small for your cause.

You've got to be a "salesman." You also have to view yourself as a salesman of ideas, and the first thing a salesman must learn is not to be slowed down by rejections. Press on to a wider circle of contacts. Don't expect a story from your first attempt. Send follow-ups, and try to establish a relationship with segments of the media so they know you and where you're coming from. Provide reporters with the raw material for stories. For example, if you want to expose unsafe playgrounds in your city, gather information on the subject from such agencies as the Consumer Product Safety Commission. (That's as easy as a call to 800-638-CPSC.) Have reports and other information on tap for the reporter you're trying to sell. Send her releases, statistics, reports, and information, and don't let up.

Continuing with the playground example, try to make contacts with experts on—and victims of—unsafe playgrounds. Journalists typically work with limited resources and do so on tight time pressures, so make it as easy as possible for a reporter to do her job. Assume the reporter might be overworked, underpaid, and uninformed, so be prepared to help in every way possible.

A case study. Some years ago, a Philadelphia schoolteacher called me to report unsafe asbestos conditions in the city's public schools. She provided some background information and contacts within the school system. This tip quickly led to my report on unsafe asbestos conditions throughout Philadelphia classrooms, eventually triggering a local scandal and a comprehensive cleanup of the asbestos. It took just a few calls by that teacher to the right reporter to get a major reform underway.

One person can make a big difference. One call, one letter, one conversation can save lives, eliminate hazards, and accomplish all kinds of other miracles. But don't give up if that one effort doesn't succeed. A high percentage of all of my exposés over the last 22 years started because one concerned person cared enough to make a call. And now more and more stories come from that one e-mail letter.

Rule Two: Get Informed, Get Organized, Get Dramatic, Get Tough

Get informed. If you want a problem corrected, learn about the issue. There's no magic formula for researching and educating yourself on any subject. Depending on the issue, you may do anything from surfing the Web to heading for a library to calling government agencies or officials.

Let's say you're having a car problem. You can see every auto complaint filed with the National Highway Traffic Safety Commission by going to its Web site: www.nhtsa.gov.

You can learn much of the standard research techniques and sources of information by looking at some of the books by information guru Matthew Lesko. For example, his book *Info-Power III*

(Visible Ink Press, 1996) is a good beginning reference source for contacts.

As one of my college professors once told me, the reason no one wants to do research is that it's tough and time-consuming work. It's not that hard if you're willing to dig in, ask questions, make some calls, check some books, etc. The information does not come down like research manna from heaven. But it is usually there if you're willing to work to find it.

Get organized. You can enhance your credibility and audience by forming an informal or formal organization to push your point of view. This effort will help open doors and make you seem more formidable and newsworthy to media organizations and others.

For example, a small neighborhood organization demands more attention and exerts more power than a bunch of individuals flailing around in different directions. If your housing development has been ripped off by the developer, form an owners' association and utilize its power. A name and a letterhead can pay big dividends.

Get dramatic. It may take more than a call or two to get the media's attention. Consider a demonstration, a picket line, or something else likely to attract attention and reporters. The media feed on controversy, conflict, and action.

If you've got a case to make, do it in the form of an official-looking report, perhaps publicized by a press conference or a mailing to media outlets. Type up a report and circulate it. If you want television coverage, make sure your news offers pictures—the standard fare of TV coverage. For example, to get back to the playground example, call a press conference at a local playground where you can demonstrate existing hazards.

If possible, you should also have on hand some "victims" and perhaps an expert on playground safety to talk to the media. In other words, try to "people-ize" your story. And after putting out a press release, be alert for follow-ups. Every time there's another playground injury, for example, recycle some of your releases and call your contacts again.

Get tough. Assert your ideas, and make it clear that you're going to fight to the finish to get them across. Just as you want politicians to know you want their attention, and that your memory extends to election time, you also have to be tough and determined when dealing with the media. Make your toughness felt with the media you're trying to sell. Let them know if you feel they are unfairly ignoring your viewpoint and your story. In an appropriate fashion, appeal beyond reporters if they won't give you a fair shake. Make sure to inform everyone involved that you're going to get your message out, and you're going to be around for the long haul.

Rule Three: Influence Public Opinion via Politicians and Government Agencies

The media are much more likely to publicize the ideas of a government official than those of an ordinary citizen. So by influencing a politician, you can sometimes influence public opinion and the media indirectly but effectively.

Know the legislators and government officials interested in your issues. Try to educate, push, and lobby them on your issue. They may propose legislation, hold hearings, or otherwise bring attention to your concerns.

This takes some know-how. You have to know the track record and interests of government agencies and legislators, and try to petition and lobby them for the kind of action you seek. I've seen many cases where a single call has triggered the introduction of legislation, and that step may lead to important publicity, hearings, and even final success.

Special Occasions

Consider the problems of the muckraker investigating the goings-on at the Ebbinger Zoo. (See "Muckraking 101" lessons.) The small town's library has an adequate reference collection, which includes encyclopedias and other standard works. A community-college library in a nearby town has a more extensive collection, but it, too, is limited in scope. Neither facility has books or periodicals that specifically examine a zoo's inner workings; the closest this researcher can get is a vacation guide with a sampling of domestic zoos and a zoology text-book that describes captive-animal behavior. A search of national newspaper indexes turns up stories about zookeeper malfeasance, ani-mal births, and bond issues to fund zoo expansion—interesting, but not particularly germane to this exercise.

Unfortunately, it's likely that a search of all that state's public libraries—including those in big cities—would produce the same unsatisfying results. The reason: This is the sort of narrow-interest topic that's usually paid attention to only by a "special" library—one maintained by a corporation, trade association, college, museum, gov-ernment agency, or the like.

In this instance, the frustrated investigator could have hit pay dirt with a trip to the library of the National Zoological Park, in Washington, D.C. The collection there—open to the public by appointment—isn't voluminous, but it's dedicated entirely to zoos, animals, and related subjects. For example, there are dozens of maga-zines and newsletters published by zoos that describe the institution's operations, complete with names of likely sources. There is a direc-tory published by the major zoological trade organization. There are materials published by an association of zookeepers. And there are government documents, annual reports, and a wide variety of other useful materials.

If all that isn't sufficient, a 20-minute drive to the National Agricultural Library, in Beltsville, Maryland, may fill in the blanks. Housed in this building is the Animal Welfare Information Center, which maintains its own collection of zoo-related materials. Between the two libraries, a researcher is likely to find answers to her ques-tions. And if she can't, there's always the Humane Society of the United States, in nearby Gaithersburg, Maryland, which has its own narrow-interest library. The librarian there may be able to help.

Of course, getting from Ebbinger to the Washington area may not be feasible. Questions can always be answered by phone. Even better, try these institutions' home pages on the Web. The Animal Welfare Information Center's Web page (www.nal.usda.gov/awic) includes copies of its newsletter, bibliographies of zoo-related materials, pro-posed legislation, and other useful materials.

There are more than 10,000 special libraries throughout the nation, and, regrettably, they're often overlooked by researchers. As a result, the most telling and valuable information may also be overlooked.

If your research has something to do with insects, for instance, the National Pest Control Association may grant you access to its library. If it won't (many special libraries are open only to organization members or the media), there are numerous other places to turn. These include collections maintained by state libraries, university entomology departments, entomological societies, Agricultural Research Service laboratories, and entomological museums, to name a few.

Of course, finding these collections can sometimes be difficult. But the following widely available reference books should help:

- *Directory of Special Libraries and Information Centers.* Published by Gale Research, the most recent edition includes e-mail addresses.

- *State and Regional Associations of the United States.* Published by Columbia Books, this provides a handy way to track down nearby trade associations.

- *Encyclopedia of Business Information Sources.* Also published by Gale Research, this volume includes trade associations, research centers, institutes, and professional societies. A CD-ROM version is also available.

- *Instant Information.* The book includes some 10,000 trade associations, think tanks, government agencies, and other sources of expert information on more than 40,000 subjects. The book was published in 1987, and many of the phone numbers are obsolete, as some of the groups have disbanded. But it still provides many worthwhile leads to obscure subjects that might otherwise be difficult to track down.

Making a Cause a Crusade

Ron Hayes did it. So did Linda Price King and Rosemary Shahan. And others did as well.

What started as one person's fight turned into an entire organization's struggle. From a single voice of discontent grew a chorus bent on change.

Making that leap to a formal organization is a long one. As a result, small groups often choose to remain informal, loose-knit coalitions. Larger groups may form unincorporated associations, which in some states carry registration requirements.

But some go the whole nine yards, forming a tax-exempt, nonprofit corporation. It's a designation that carries not only a certain cachet, but also decided benefits: The organization is not taxed, there are postal and other discounts, and because donations are tax deductible, benefactors are often easier to attract.

There are potential drawbacks, however, including IRS restrictions on how money may be earned and spent. In addition, incorporation costs can be significant, as can annual accountant fees. Articles of incorporation and bylaws must be filed, and annual reports are just one component of the administrative burden. Throw in staffing, training volunteers, paying the rent, and coping with unanticipated nightmares like auto accidents or litigious ex-employees, and the notion of solo muckraking can look all the more appealing.

But if the idea of a 501(c)(3) designation still has appeal, there are some valuable resources that will help you understand how to incorporate a nonprofit and run it successfully. Most libraries have books on the subject. One well-regarded guide is Anthony Mancuso's *How to Form a Nonprofit Corporation* (Nolo Press), which includes detailed instructions for obtaining federal tax exemptions. The book also includes boilerplate forms for the articles of incorporation and bylaws on disk.

There are also some good online guides that offer the fundamentals of starting and running a nonprofit organization. One good one is the Internet Nonprofit Center, a project of the Evergreen State Society, in Seattle. The site www.nonprofit-info.org/npofaq/keywords/1l.html includes sections on such topics as:

- How do I incorporate an organization as a nonprofit?

- Do I need a lawyer to do this? How much should I pay?

- What actual documents do I need? Which filings come first?

- What about getting a nonprofit bulk-mail permit?

Along with this guide, the INC has many other tutorials of value to nonprofits accessible from their Web site.

Muckraking 101
Lesson Six: Going Public

Congratulations are in order. The questionable activities have been pieced together. Those involved in this scheme to profit from the sale of municipally owned zoo animals have been exposed. Enough documentation has been collected to substantiate the questionable business dealing. All of which begs the question that was asked at the beginning of this pursuit: Now what?

Investigative journalists doing the same work have an obvious edge: When all is said and done, they have outlets for their work that guarantee the story exposure. But citizen muckrakers usually don't. After all, many of their investigations were launched only because the press wasn't paying attention.

A report piecing together the story is written. The facts are checked thoroughly, and documents substantiating every claim are placed in a briefing book. Copies of the most notable documents are attached to the report. A news release is written announcing a press conference. The release is mailed to print and broadcast reporters. Follow-up calls to these journalists are made the next day. A copy of the announcement is delivered to the daybook editor at the local wire-service office.

The press conference is held on a Tuesday morning, a few hours before the mayor's weekly press briefing. It's staged in a public park directly behind the zoo. Reporters arriving at the news conference are asked to sign in and state their affiliation. Each is given a news release that encapsulates the major points of the report. Each also receives a copy of the prepared remarks that are delivered by the report's author.

The remarks are brief and to the point, and then the floor is opened up to questions. A dry run, with anticipated questions, was held the previous evening. Other members of the citizen advisory board that has zoo oversight, whose support had been solicited in the course of the investigation, are on hand to also answer questions.

Later that afternoon, the mayor is asked about the allegations at his news conference. He's well prepared with a response. The reason: In this state, when a politician's financial-disclosure forms are requested for inspection, the subject of the investigation is notified. As a result, the mayor had been tipped off in advance, and thus forewarned he had cranked up his public-relations machine. He labeled the report's author an animal-rights zealot, reiterated his faith in the zoo's director, and promised to have an audit conducted to assure the town's citizens that no funny business was going on in his administration.

Reporters pressed him to explain the report's findings, but he side-stepped their questions. Finally, he was asked to explain the large campaign contribution from the out-of-state petting zoo, and he claimed to have no knowledge of it. In fact, he said he never heard of the place and had never met its owner or employees.

No one could prove otherwise, except for a reporter from the area's largest daily, who had obtained copies of the mayor's **cellular-phone records** by filing a **FOIA request**. Those records showed calls to that petting zoo, as well as to Tim Overpeck's home.

Checkmate. Front page. Nightly news.

Of course, a muckraker's quest doesn't always turn out this way. But as long as this one was hypothetical, it may as well end with a bang.

CHAPTER EIGHT

Opposition Research

The pen isn't the only communications tool that's mightier than the sword. There's also the video camera, which in the right hands can produce some very special effects—for instance, making a mountain of trash disappear.

Nine years after John and Terri Moore arrived in Center Point, Indiana, the couple finally moved out of town and into their more rural dream house. The house sits on twenty-five acres, a quarter of which is covered by a lake. Deer, raccoons, and coyotes are among the wildlife that roam the Moores' property. There's a great blue heron that calls the lake home, and for a while each year it's joined by migrating Canada geese. The house is modest, but it's the place where the couple wanted to raise their two children.

"We used to drive by, and we'd say, 'We'll live there one day,'" Terri says. "We wanted to raise our children with the sounds of nature and small-town values you can't get in the city."

Towns don't get much smaller than Center Point, whose population of 293 is slightly higher than the 1990 census. It's an out-of-the-way stretch of farmland an hour west of Indianapolis, not far from the Illinois line. The drive to Center Point from the Hoosier State capital is almost entirely a cruise-control jaunt along Interstate 70, where at times the only other vehicles seem to be trucks hauling cattle to market.

This sort of out-of-the-way, rural living may have held great appeal for Terri and John Moore, but eighteen months after relocating to their new home, the dream turned nightmarish. The reason: a proposal surfaced to build a landfill directly behind their home. There was already a small, privately owned town dump just 1,700 feet from their property, and another, they feared, not only would jeopardize their tranquility but also might compromise the environment. So the couple initiated a battle to keep the second facility from opening.

Then things really turned ominous. In the midst of their anti-dump fight, the owner of the existing landfill called to offer the Moores a financial contribution—his way, he said, of supporting their effort. And by the way, he added, it's likely that a few semi-trailers will soon begin hauling trash into his facility, and those numbers may grow over time. Terri Moore hung up the phone with a sense that something horrible was about to happen.

Ordinarily, only cars and pickups and a few small trucks traveled the narrow dirt road that leads to the ninety acres on which that landfill sat. Terri Moore told townspeople of her conversation and the impending arrival of the big rigs, but no one believed her. On the following Monday, however, the skepticism quickly evaporated: The first of the semis rolled in, and over the subsequent weeks and months the number pushed up toward fifty a day.

The tiny town of Center Point had become a magnet for drivers hauling forty-foot loads of trash, many of the vehicles adorned with license plates from Northeastern and Mid-Atlantic states, primarily New York, New Jersey, and Pennsylvania. And if the residents thought the situation couldn't get worse, they soon learned otherwise: Two other companies were looking at adjoining land for another dump, and a trio of firms had optioned a square mile for—what else?— yet more landfill space.

In Indiana, it turned out, there was gold in the garbage.

If the idea of hauling truckloads of trash from the Eastern Seaboard to the nation's heartland seems odd, consider the economics: In 1989, when the Center Point trash caravan was moving into high gear, the cost of dumping a ton of garbage in Indiana was $10, while in the New York/New Jersey area it was $100 to $150. It was therefore a lot cheaper for Easterners to haul the waste out of state, particularly if the trailer could be filled with something else for the return trip. In fact, the joke was that it would be cheaper to FedEx garbage to west-ern Indiana than to dump it on the East Coast.

But the residents of Center Point weren't laughing. And neither were they giving in to the invasion without a fight.

For Terri and John Moore, the battle would be waged on two fronts. On one front was the proposed new facility, which would sit just a hundred feet from the couple's property and, they feared, would contaminate their lake. On the other was the invasion of the semis with their unwanted imports, including asbestos and medical waste.

"We rode a huge roller coaster," Terri says. "We always had one or the other looming over our head."

The goal in the first fight was to demonstrate that the area was geologically unsound—that disposing of waste on this site might wreak environmental havoc. Terri and the citizens' group she helped organize pinned their hopes on a state law that decreed that a landfill couldn't be positioned over an abandoned mine. There were indeed defunct coal mines in the area, but proving that one may once have operated beneath this turf proved difficult.

Terri Moore likens the hunt for such evidence to piecing together a big puzzle. The campaign was built on a search for quantifiable facts and data, and group members would regularly convene in someone's living room to report their findings. Reporters were invited to the meetings from the outset, so the group developed a rapport with the media and generated valuable press coverage for its cause.

The search for maps was a major component of the effort, but the cartographic documents examined at governmental offices showed no evidence of abandoned mines. Then the trail unexpectedly led to a church secretary whose late husband had been a geologist. He had apparently kept books from the previous century filled with local maps.

The books had been sent to the local courthouse, but no one there could find them. Moore tracked them down to another Indiana town and then traveled an hour and a half to view them. The volumes included original cloth maps and certified copies of other maps show-ing the precise locations of mines—including one beneath the proposed landfill. But Moore didn't stop there. She researched other sites in every direction and was able to show where the state had repaired mineshafts that had caved in. It was the proof she needed. She had hit the mother lode.

But while Terri Moore had one battle under control, the war raged on. There were, of course, those tractor-trailers to contend with.

On the very Monday that the trucks first arrived, Moore grabbed her 35mm camera and went off to shoot some film. She realized immediately that without documentation, outsiders probably wouldn't believe what was happening in her town. So she enlisted the help of three or four neighbors, who within a week were outfitted with pads, pencils, binoculars, and tape recorders. From their lawn chairs beside the road, the "Dump Patrol," as they came to be known, dutifully recorded what they witnessed.

The citizens' group also gave immediate attention to attracting the news media. They invited reporters to their meetings and, before adjourning, a definite time was set for the next session. That tactic gave journalists ample warning, and the group subsequently reminded them of the meetings by telephone.

In addition, members of Moore's group tried to attend events that were likely to receive media coverage, including the "cracker-barrel" meetings – a Hoosier tradition – in which voters discuss local issues with their state legislators. Within a few weeks of the invasion of the semis, Terri Moore also had some of her photos enlarged for a three-minute presentation to a committee of the Indiana legislature. She was uncomfortable speaking in public, but she was determined to describe the invasion underway in her community. The room was packed, there was a full agenda, and no one knew the woman from Center Point who was first to take the floor. "The entire room went from bustling to silence when I was speaking," Moore recalls. "I thought: I know I did it."

Moore's testimony brought attention to her cause, and on its heels she and her cohorts stepped up their campaign. Moore soon shelled out a thousand dollars for a camcorder, and about seventy-five residents volunteered to record the comings and goings of the trucks, documenting everything from time and date to license-plate numbers, trucking-company names, and tractor-trailer serial numbers. A local dealer donated a small trailer for the sleuths to work from. For ten hours a day, six days a week, the citizens of Center Point maintained a fourteen-month vigil. They missed only two days during that period, when the trailer's furnace failed and the sub-zero winter temperatures posed a health hazard.

The proliferation of low-priced camcorders has made the use of video an increasingly popular—and effective—technique for citizen muckrakers. Some have used it for advocacy building, while others have documented everything from dolphin slaughter on tuna-fishing boats to deplorable living conditions in public housing. For Moore, video was a tool of empowerment that gave her cause wide-eyed attention.

Moore felt strongly that a voluminous tape archive was essential, because it would provide the only record of culpability in the event of an environmental mishap. It was also in keeping with the group's strategy of documenting every fact and being able to substantiate each claim. If they told reporters that fifty trucks a day were rolling down their roads, they had supporting evidence. Because they were so credible, reporters looked to them for information. In addition, the home video was made to order for television; segments of the tape were featured on local and national newscasts.

In addition to the video surveillance, Moore followed a paper trail that led her to a startling revelation: Among those affiliated with the landfill was a New Jersey trash baron whom authorities had connected to the Genovese-Gigante crime family. Moore's research effort was aided by local reporters, who conducted invaluable searches for her on Nexis, the online news library, and made other documents available. In return, news organizations received well-documented evidence that was useful to their stories. In fact, Moore always had documents certified to ensure that reporters would never doubt their authenticity.

Center Point residents were also helped in their efforts by some unlikely confidential sources: truck drivers and landfill employees they befriended. For example, the sleuths quickly realized that the trucks bringing in trash were in many instances "backhauling"—that is, picking up loads for the return trip. The trucks that carried garbage west, it turned out, were carrying slaughtered carcasses and other food products east. One driver even stopped to show the Center Point spies his trailer: The wooden floor was covered with an inch of pine-oil dis-infectant, but it was nonetheless overrun with maggots. He admitted that on previous trips the food he delivered was swarming with flies.

There were no prohibitions against backhauling, but Moore tracked down a U.S. Representative from New Jersey who was inter-ested in legislation that would regulate the practice. Her video provided graphic evidence of the maggot-filled trucks—something that other Members of Congress had previously dismissed as an unfounded rumor.

This backhauling issue provided a weapon for the Center Point residents. A legislative remedy to outlaw the dumping wasn't feasi-ble, because the courts had ruled that shipments of garbage constituted interstate commerce, and the U.S. Constitution limits the power of states to interfere with such commerce. But in late 1992, Indiana state legislators passed a law declaring that anyone trucking in garbage had to wait two weeks before backhauling other goods from the state. And a more enforceable law required anyone trucking in garbage to show that it originated at a licensed waste-transfer station. The legislation immediately stopped the inflow of illegal shipments, which brought a small measure of peace to the besieged community.

The landfill was later sold, and the ongoing bad publicity even-tually forced the new owners to stop accepting long-haul waste. Then, in early 1994, the traffic slowed, and one day it just stopped. "Everyone held their breath and said, 'Is it really over?' We weren't quite sure," Moore says.

Apparently, it is over. The former dump is now a grassy hill beset by erosion; the owner must monitor the land for thirty years. The clos-est landfill is a twenty-minute drive away. Copies of all the Center Point group's records were handed over to the state in the hope they'll be archived—ammunition for future generations if the same issue should ever arise again. And the townspeople who waged this effort have developed close friendships with one another.

As for Terri and John Moore, they still live in their dream house. Terri recounts the tale almost nonchalantly, but then catches herself. "I look back and think: I can't believe I did that," she says.

Ask the Experts

You need background information on a company, but a check of newspaper indexes and other obvious sources reveals nothing. As a result, your investigative task appears to have the makings of an arduous, time-consuming one. But Larry Zilliox, Jr., author of *The Opposition Research Handbook: A Guide to Political Investigations*, says there may be an easy shortcut:

"My best tip is, first, put effort into finding people who have done the work already. For everyone doing something, there are two people watching them. The anti-widget people know all about the widget manufacturers. You can spend two weeks investigating the widget people, or you can go to the anti-widget people.

"In other words, look 180 degrees opposite for a real source of information."

And how do you find those experts who may have already done the work? Here are some valuable sources:

- **National Trade and Professional Associations of the United States.** This annual reference book, published by Columbia Books, lists trade associations, professional societies, technical organizations, and labor unions with national memberships. The primary index is arranged alphabetically by organization name; one of the five subsidiary indexes is arranged by subject of interest. If it's not available in your library, search it for free online at: www.d-net.com/columbia/pip00003/search.htm.

The following trio of volumes published by Gale Research will help you track down experts in just about any field of interest:

- *Research Centers Directory.* The source for those affiliated with universities and independent nonprofit organizations.

- *Research Services Directory.* This volume, which covers private-sector firms and individuals aligned with for-profit institutions, will help you track down someone to do anything from radioactivity testing to soil analysis.

- *Government Research Directory.* The source for experts at government-funded programs.

If you're searching for a lawyer with expertise in a particular area, your best source is the *Martindale-Hubbell Law Directory*. This multi-volume set is available in many libraries. If you have Internet access, the directory may be searched online for free. The search engine will let you find individual attorneys or firms with expertise in anything from energy to immigration. The address is www.martindale.com. West Legal Directory provides another source on the Web: www.lawoffice.com.

Nonprofit organizations with interests similar to yours may have already done legwork you'll find valuable. One of the best ways to find like-minded groups—both in the United States and overseas—is via the Institute for Global Communications, which was formed in 1987. Contact IGC at: Presidio Building 1012, First Floor, Torney Avenue, P.O. Box 29904, San Francisco, CA 94129-0904; (415) 561-6100. The East Coast office is at 1731 Connecticut Avenue, NW, Suite 400, Washington, D.C. 20009; (202) 588-5070.

IGC's Web site also provides an easy way to find hundreds of public-interest organizations and links to their home pages. The Internet address is www.igc.org/igc/gateway/members/index.html.

Super Sleuths

Talk about tempting: A Walkman-like device will let you listen in on the park-bench conversations of a man whose company is suspected of illegally dumping sludge in the woods behind your home. But there's a nagging question: If you do "accidentally" eavesdrop, would you also be breaking the law?

Muckrakers can certainly employ technology—and other more mundane snooping methods—to their advantage. For example, if you believe that a company's trash may contain important clues about the nature of its operations, then Dumpster-diving you should go. The Supreme Court has ruled that the Constitution does not prohibit the search of garbage placed *outside* someone's premises. So if the can's on the curb, you can legally make off with the discarded computer print-outs.

In some instances, however, less traditional forms of reporting can run afoul of the law. As a result, you need to familiarize yourself with applicable statutes before deciding to impersonate James Bond.

A good resource for tracking down information on these laws is the Brechner Center, a unit of the College of Journalism and Communications at the University of Florida. The center's *State Media Law Sourcebook* provides a listing of media-law sources by state. The Brechner Center can be reached at (352) 392-2273. Its Web site also provides a state-by-state directory of relevant legal guides, complete with ordering information. The Internet address is www.jou.ufl.edu /brechner/srcbk.htm.

Another excellent source is *Tapping Officials' Secrets*, published by the Reporters Committee for Freedom of the Press. The laws of each state are covered in a separate volume. Ordering information for these guides and the Committee's other publications is available from the organization at 1815 N. Ft. Meyer Drive, Suite 900, Arlington, VA 22209; (800) 336-4243 or (703) 807-2100.

In addition, the Reporters Committee maintains a useful Web site (www.rcfp.org) with advice on such things as a citizen's right to tape conversations. Here are some highlights:

- **Consent to tape a conversation:** Generally, you may record, film, broadcast, or amplify any conversation where all the parties to it consent. It is always legal to tape or film a face-to-face interview when your recorder or camera is in plain view; the consent of all parties is presumed in these instances. As a general rule, federal law requires only one-party consent to the recording and disclosure of a telephone conversation. All but twelve states permit you to record a conversation without informing the other parties you are doing so. Those that forbid it are California, Connecticut, Delaware, Florida, Illinois, Maryland, Massachusetts, Michigan, Montana, New Hampshire, Pennsylvania, and Washington. When recording or disclosing an interstate telephone call, err on the side of caution. The safest strategy is to assume that the stricter state law will apply.

- **Cellular phone conversations:** The 1986 Electronic Communications Privacy Act (the federal wiretap law) makes it illegal to intentionally intercept cellular phone calls, and to possess or divulge the contents of any intercepted conversation.

- **Hidden cameras:** The use of hidden cameras or other forms of surreptitious filming can lead to legal charges such as trespass. In many states, the same statutes governing wiretapping also cover the use of hidden cameras. However, a few states have adopted laws specific to the use of video and still cameras. For example, some states prohibit the installation or use of cameras in private places—that is, places where a person may reasonably expect to be safe from unauthorized surveillance.

Sly vs. Sly

A former reporter who would prefer to remain nameless (i.e., he was speaking "on background") tells this story of his experience covering the Federal Trade Commission. He was following an important issue for a weekly magazine and was tipped off to the supposed existence of some revealing documents. The only way to get hold of these documents was via a Freedom of Information Act request, but there was a problem: The FTC kept a loose-leaf binder in its public reference room that contained copies of all FOIA requests, and filing a FOIA might therefore let other reporters in on his secret. What's more, he worried, the daily newspapers might receive the documents simultaneously, permitting them to get the story into print before his weekly magazine ran it. His "scoop" would be attached to someone else's byline.

So he appealed to the agency's FOIA officer, who said that he sympathized, but nothing could be done to ensure the reporter—or anyone else—an exclusive. So the journalist offered a compromise: He would draft the FOIA letter in a foreign language, and the FOIA officer could both fill the request and put the letter in the publicly accessible binder. But the increasingly weary FOIA officer said he would send the letter to the State Department for translation and then put it in the binder along with the original. The reporter countered that he'd steal the English version from the FOIA book, and the bureaucrat replied that he'd have the thief arrested.

Incarceration seemed like a high price to pay for a magazine story, so the reporter finally worked out another strategy: He handwrote his FOIA request—in his worst possible penmanship—on lined notebook paper rather than on his magazine's letterhead. He figured that other reporters would go right by the sloppily crafted page and not stop to read it. A brilliant strategy, except for one thing: His tipster turned out to be not particularly well informed. The FOIA request produced no documents. No scoop. No story. The only positive outcome was that there was no jail time.

It's hard to keep your FOIA requests secret. In fact, it's often difficult to keep any investigation under wraps. Call an office for information, and the person on the other end may mention the conversation to a coworker, who in turn tells someone with a friend at the company under scrutiny. Before long, that company may be doing an investigation of you. Or it may search out copies of the documents you've received—a way to know what the opposition has learned.

Consider how easy it has become to conduct at least some of this opposition research. If you're unable to regularly consult the FOIA-request binder at the Federal Trade Commission, you can snoop on others via the commercially available *FTC FOIA Log*. (It and *Antitrust FOIA Log*—along with a thousand other publications—are also available online from the Dialog Corporation at www.dialog.com.) This newsletter lists the requestor's name and address, the materials being sought, and the control number assigned by the agency.

In December 1995, for example, an attorney with the New York firm of Davis & Gilbert filed a request for any FTC correspondence with the Tutor Time franchise—a Florida-based operator of child-care learning centers. If Tutor Time didn't know that a law firm was snooping into its affairs, the newsletter could have tipped it off. And a quick Internet search would have revealed some key information not only about the firm but also about the attorney filing the FOIA: where and when he was born, his educational background, where he was admitted to practice law, and that his areas of practice included advertising law. Armed with that information, Tutor Time could have initiated its own investigation.

There are other publications that print FOIA requests sent to agencies. Some secretaries of state are now posting FOIA requests on their Web sites. The Washington, D.C.-based firm FOIA Group (www.foia.com) has introduced Reverse FOIA Online, a subscription service that publishes the FOIA logs of many federal agencies. This trend will no doubt escalate.

In some jurisdictions, the subject of a records request is automatically notified of the request. In King County, Washington, for example, the Board of Ethics maintains financial-disclosure forms for all elected officials, board and commission members, and top county employees. If a citizen asks for a copy of someone's disclosure form, the Board of Ethics notifies that county employee. Furthermore, that employee has fourteen days to ask the court to block release of the information.

So don't assume that your efforts are always secret. This information shouldn't deter you, but it should make you sensitive to the fact that the subject of your investigation may know what you're up to. In fact, he or she may be returning the favor.

Lights, Camera, Reaction

Print used to be the only game in town for citizen muckrakers, whose efforts invariably ended with a report, newsletter, or study. But activists such as Terri Moore prove that other media can be equally effective investigative tools. Sometimes, in fact, they're far more so.

Video can be a particularly compelling medium, although most individuals or organizations setting out on an investigative project don't even consider the possibility of using video to augment their reporting. As a result, the chance to release their findings in an alternative format is lost from the get-go.

One nonprofit organization that teaches groups how to use video is the Benton Foundation, based in Washington, D.C. Consider the ideas of executive director Larry Kirkman on why activists ought to start paying closer attention to the possibilities that video offers:

> Citizen activists are using video to help reframe social problems, attract mass-media coverage, and mobilize grassroots support. Videos

are a modern-day pamphlet, dropped off in door-to-door canvassing, distributed on street corners, used for intimate appeal in boardrooms and community forums. Whether for portraying hazardous working conditions, preventing an incinerator in a neighborhood, or outlining a strategy for community development, advocacy video is a powerful tool for activists to make their own case, outside the restrictive formats and prejudices of television, and to address the audiences they need to reach.

Videos offer visual evidence, for example, of a corporation's toxic dumping or a landlord's neglect of rental housing. Videos give a voice to experience that is denied on the evening news, offering the testimony and the storytelling that verifies urgent messages of need, visualizing problems, and inspiring confidence in the solutions activists propose. By marshaling an argument, modeling a conversation, and illustrating data, videos have helped viewers gain the understanding to master complex issues and take on the toughest opposition.

To take advantage of the potential of video for advocacy, activists have to discard the models of 16mm institutional film, broadcast news, and television documentaries. They have to question their assumptions about what a film is good for and who can be a producer. With the emerging technologies of desktop computer editing and graphics, and low-cost, high-quality cameras, the tools are becoming more widely accessible and the production processes more flexible. With the introduction of video on the Internet, activists will have the opportunity to add the power of visual representation to Web sites, and to fulfill the promise of interactive public-service multimedia knowledge centers. Such centers can become a community media bank, in the way we have come to approve of the community development bank. Instead of the annual organizational film or occasional television coverage, we could see in our communities a flow of visual communications that encourages new forms of interaction and enlarges political debate.

The Benton Foundation has produced a series of guides to help organizations make better use of video. One is *Producing Change: How Nonprofit Organizations Use Video and Television To Create Social Change*, which chronicles innovative uses of video by activists and nonprofits. The foundation has also produced the handbook *Making*

Video, which offers instructions on producing video. Included with the report is a videotape that illustrates the text.

Details are available from the Benton Foundation, 1800 K Street, NW, Second Floor, Washington, D.C. 20006; (202) 638-5770. A text version of *Producing Change* is available at no cost on the foundation's Web site: www.benton.org/Library.

If you need only some basic tips about shooting Terri Moore-type video, here's a guide from David Weiner at the Benton Foundation:

- **Look and *listen* where you shoot.** You may have to rely on the camera's built-in microphone; keep in mind how the video is going to sound as well as how it will look. Whatever you are recording, whether it is a conversation or a sporting event, a speech or a party, it is important to take the audio seriously. Is the microphone close enough? Is it pointed in the right direction? Are things happening off-camera that need to be heard? Common sense will often be all that is needed, but care must be taken.

- **The thing you are recording is not the only thing you *should* be recording.** If you are at a rally watching a speech, your eyes are not fixed on the speaker constantly. You find yourself looking around at others to see how they're reacting, to take the measure of the crowd's size, or even just to see what the setting is like. Use the same logic while videotaping. Staying on a single shot of a speaker, a factory puffing smoke, or a person at work will make your video virtually unwatchable. Concentrate, of course, on the main element, but think about shooting all the things that will help tell the complete story.

- **Vary the shot, but do so wisely.** Along with the previous advice, it's important to shoot your subject in close, medium, and wide shots. But don't zoom in and out constantly. Frame a shot and stay there; then, at an appropriate time, change the shot, stay there, and repeat.

- **Either plan to edit or don't overshoot.** Movies have shooting ratios that vary from 40-to-1 up to 150-to-1—sometimes even more. That means that for every second used in the finished film, anywhere from 40 to 150 (or whatever number) of seconds are shot. Most videos, on the other hand, are shot in a ratio of 1 to 1. As a result, people generally have to sit through a lot of mediocre material to get to the best moments. That's the primary reason why people just stop taping after a while. If you're not going to edit, then be careful with the amount of material you actually record.

- **Practice**. It will take time and a lot of trial and error to learn how to shoot smoothly, to use light properly, to get good sound, and, especially, to make good judgments. Take the time. It'll be worth it.

Follow the Money

When it comes to investigating the finances of politicians, there's no such thing as one-stop shopping. While the Federal Election Commission maintains a variety of campaign-finance reports, including details of federal candidates' spending and campaign contributions received, it is the Secretary of the Senate and the Clerk of the House that keep record of such things as Members of Congress's stock ownership and outside income. If you want the lowdown on a state elected official, in most instances the documents reside with the Secretary of State. County and local government offices are other stops on the campaign-finance itinerary. Here are some tips for narrowing the search:

- The Federal Election Commission (800-424-9530, or www.fec.gov) maintains records on candidates, political action committees, party and other committees, and individual contributors to campaigns (since 1989, those who gave $200 or more in a calendar year). All of these documents are publicly available for inspection and copying at the FEC's Washington, D.C., headquarters. Computerized search indexes make the location of documents fairly effortless. On the FEC's Web site, its Image/Query System (www.fec.gov/1996/sdrindex.htm) allows you to see photographic images of the reports filed with the Commission—down to the candidate or treasurer's signature. And a Directory of Federal Offices (www.fec.gov/pubrec/feddir.htm) gives links to other federal agencies and national associations that deal with election issues, as well as their telephone numbers and mailing addresses.

- In most states, election-related records are scattered among a number of offices under the umbrella of the secretary of state's office. Typically, a state board of elections will house state campaign-finance reports, while a board of ethics often has responsibility for keeping state personal financial reports and lobbying reports.

- County record-keeping systems often mirror those of the state. In addition to administering elections, a supervisor of elections may also oversee candidates' campaign-finance reports and financial-disclosure reports. Meanwhile, a county board of ethics often handles the collection of annual financial-disclosure forms filed by elected county officials, county-council employees, board and commission members, and those officials who participate in the awarding of contracts.

One convenient way to find the location of records is the Federal Election Commission's Combined Federal/State Disclosure Directory. For ordering information, contact the agency's Public Disclosure Division at (800) 424-9530. The most recent annual directory is also available on the FEC's Web site at www.fec.gov/pubrec/cfsdd.htm.

There are also many nongovernmental sources that can help you track down and analyze campaign-related documents. The Center for Responsive Politics is a Washington-based nonpartisan, nonprofit research group that specializes in the role of money in federal elections. CRP has a variety of publications that may prove useful. Information is available at (202) 857-0044, or by e-mail at info@crp.org. In addition, there are a great many searchable databases on the organization's Web site (www.opensecrets.org), including some that allow you to search by donor as well as by candidate. And here at The Center for Public Integrity, our 50 States Project (www.publicintegrity.org/50States_main.html) can tell you how to find out about state legislators' private financial interests and activities, and potential conflicts of interest.

Finally, the secretary of state's office not only maintains information about public officials, but it's also the source for documents about corporations. Secretaries of state are increasingly mounting such information on their Web sites, offering online searches of everything from campaign-finance reports to details on limited partnerships, fictitious names, and Uniform Commercial Code filings. Here is a secretary-of-state electronic contact list:

State	Phone	E-mail and/or Web Site
AL	(334) 242-7205	www.sos.state.al.us
AK	(907) 465-3520	**Fran_Ulmer@Gov.state.ak.us** www.gov.state.ak.us/ltgov
AZ	(602) 542-4285	sosadmin@mail.sosaz.com www.sosaz.com
AR	(501) 682-1010	spriest@sosmail.state.ar.us sos.state.ar.us
CA	(916) 653-7244	bjones@ss.ca.gov www.ss.ca.gov
CO	(303) 894-2200	sos.admin1@state.co.us **www.state.co.us/gov_dir/sos/index.html**
CT	(860) 566-2739	harland.henry@po.state.ct.us www.state.ct.us/sots
DE	(302) 577-3095	www.state.de.us/sos
D.C.	(202) 727-6306	
FL	(850) 414-5500	secretary@mail.dos.state.fl.us www.dos.state.fl.us
GA	(404) 656-2881	sosweb@sos.state.ga.us www.sos.state.ga.us
HI	(808) 586-0255	www.hawaii.gov/icsd/test2.htm
ID	(208) 334-2300	sosinfo@idsos.state.id.us www.idsos.state.id.us

IL	(217) 782-2201	secwhite@ccgate.sos.state.il.us
		www.sos.state.il.us
IN	(317) 232-6531	www.state.in.us/sos
IA	(515) 281-8993	sos@sos.state.ia.us
		www.sos.state.ia.us
KS	(785) 296-4564	RonT@ssmail.wpo.state.ks.us
		www.ink.org/public/sos
KY	(502) 564-3490	jbrown@mail.state.ky.us
		www.sos.state.ky.us
LA	(225) 342-4479	kaiserb@sec.state.la.us
		www.sec.state.la.us
ME	(207) 626-8400	sos.office@state.me.us
		www.state.me.us/sos/sos.htm
MD	(410) 974-5521	mdsos@sos.state.md.us
		www.sos.state.md.us
MA	(617) 727-7030	www.state.ma.us/sec/index.htm
MI	(517) 373-2510	www.sos.state.mi.us
MN	(612) 296-2803	secretary.state@state.mn.us
		www.state.mn.us/ebranch/sos
MS	(601) 359-1350	administrator@sos.state.ms.us
		www.sos.state.ms.us
MO	(573) 751-4936	sosmain@mail.sos.state.mo.us
		mosl.sos.state.mo.us
MT	(406) 444-2034	sos@mt.gov
		www.mt.gov/sos/index.htm
NE	(402) 471-2554	sos04@nol.org
		www.nol.org/home/SOS
NV	(775) 684-5708	sosinfo@govmail.state.nv.us
		sos.state.nv.us
NH	(603) 271-3242	www.state.nh.us/sos

NJ	(609) 777-0884	feedback@sos.state.nj.us www.state.nj.us/state
NM	(505) 827-3600	web.state.nm.us
NY	(518) 474-0050	info@dos.state.ny.us www.dos.state.ny.us
NC	(919) 733-4143	gjeter@mail.secstate.state.nc.us www.state.nc.us/secstate
ND	(701) 328-2992	sos@state.nd.us www.state.nd.us/sec
OH	(614) 466-3910	blackwell@sos.state.oh.us www.state.oh.us/sos
OK	(405) 521-3911	www.state.ok.us/~sos
OR	(503) 986-1523	executive-office@sosinet.sos.state.or.us www.sos.state.or.us
PA	(717) 787-6458	www.dos.state.pa.us
RI	(401) 222-2357	jlangevin@sec.state.ri.us www.sec.state.ri.us
SC	(803) 734-2170	
SD	(605) 773-3537	sdsos@state.sd.us www.state.sd.us/state/executive/sos /sos.htm
TN	(615) 741-2819	rdarnell@mail.state.tn.us www.state.tn.us/sos/soshmpg.htm
TX	(512) 463-5701	dwright@sos.state.tx.us www.sos.state.tx.us
UT	(801) 538-1000	kajones@gov.state.ut.us **www.governor.state.ut.us/menu/html /Lt_Gover.html**
VT	(802) 828-2363	dmarko@sec.state.vt.us www.sec.state.vt.us

CITIZEN MUCKRAKING

VA	(804) 786-2441	www.soc.state.va.us
WA	(360) 753-7121	secstate@www.wa.gov
		www.wa.gov/sec/sechome.htm
WV	(304) 558-6000	wvsos@secretary.state.wv.us
		www.state.wv.us/sos
WI	(608) 266-8888	badger.state.wi.us/agencies/sos
WY	(307) 777-7378	secofstate@state.wy.us
		soswy.state.wy.us

CHAPTER NINE

Brave New Worlds

For a quarter-century, attorney Richard Means searched for a way to put issue-oriented data into the hands of fellow Chicagoans. Then he got himself a computer and a modem, and the next thing he knew his quest had ended in a unique little patch of cyberspace.

Richard Means had a brainstorm: He would gather and publish a wide range of information about the government of Illinois that was not otherwise publicly accessible. He would make available data collected by state and local agencies that rarely, if ever, found its way into print. He would explore issues of the day in an entirely new fashion—give every candidate an in-depth question-naire, for example, and then simply publish the answers in their entirety. There would be no analysis of the replies, no abridged high-lights, just unedited statements that would, he hoped, permit voters and political organizations to make more informed decisions.

The underlying philosophy of his idea, says Means, was that an informed electorate would affect the political system in a fashion that would permit the public to get what it wanted. And what better way to inform that electorate than to lay out timely, in-depth information not readily available from newspapers or other media? As a voter-education tool, this innovative project was perfect.

Well, not quite.

Means's idea, which he hatched in 1971 with a group of like-minded acquaintances, did have pitfalls. Most notable was the matter of cost: Collecting, collating, and processing large amounts of data was expensive, and with the photocopy machine still a novelty in most offices, reproduction charges were equally prohibitive. Add to this the high price of distribution, and Means was forced to squirrel away his project in the "unfeasible" file. Instead, he says, he decided to work on ways to ensure honest elections—a venture that complemented his budding career as an election-law attorney.

Fast forward a quarter-century. Richard Means's résumé now boasted a long list of achievements related to consumer issues, election fraud, Freedom of Information Act litigation, and the development of legislation on behalf of public-interest groups. But the fiftysomething Chicagoan, who cheerfully applied to himself the anachronistic label of civil-liberties attorney, was still pondering the feasibility of his long-discarded idea. Means had briefly dusted off the concept in 1981, after a five-year stint as an assistant state's attorney for Cook County, Illinois, but again concluded that money was an insurmountable hurdle.

This time, however, he thought he had the answer.

With rudimentary desktop publishing skills and a fax machine at his disposal, Means realized that high production and distribution costs were no longer stumbling blocks. Add the World Wide Web to the mix, and he had a way to dramatically expand both his reach and the quantity of his offerings. In short order, the Public Access Project was finally born.

The idea behind this nonprofit civic association, run by Means from his law office, is simple: Enhance public empowerment by pressing Illinois state and local officials to obey the laws requiring open government. "Citizen knowledge is truly citizen power, best maximized by expanding the effectiveness of the state's adequate, but inadequately enforced, laws," Means writes in his organization's mission statement.

To accomplish that goal, Means devised a two-pronged strategy: (1) File Freedom of Information Act requests on behalf of citizens and the media and (2) use computers to collect, analyze, and publish the public information held by governments and the public disclosures made by lobbyists, office holders, and candidates. Push hard enough, Means figured, and his group could entice—perhaps even embarrass—

public officials into making available all types of documents not ordinarily released. And should the keepers of such information refuse to make it public, Means knew that his legal experience provided the sort of advantage that others before him may have lacked: "When patient and polite requests do not result in prompt and full disclosure," the mission statement adds, "Public Access has both the resources and the readiness to litigate to enforce the laws."

Starting an organization can be daunting, but new technologies gave Means the wherewithal to move ahead quickly. "When I found out how easy it was to use this technology, I decided that now I could launch Public Access," he says. "I could go to people and say, 'Give me a little money, agree to do some research, be on a board, give me advice.' It's easily doable to provide information that reporters and activists want to see or candidates want to see about their opponents. We can, in effect, leverage governmental reform."

Means hardly pioneered the concept of Internet-based publishing, which has of course become a favored distribution tool of universities, libraries, government agencies, interest groups, and just about anyone else with something—no matter how brilliant or banal—to share with the world. But many of the digital warriors who made a mad dash for the Web were already technologically savvy. Means, by contrast, considered the operator's headset he wore while taking telephone calls to be pretty high-tech.

That meant having to find someone to build, maintain, and update the Public Access Web site—a potentially large expense. Or it meant that Means, whose project was designated a relatively meager out-of-pocket budget, needed to don an unfamiliar hat.

The prospects of learning Hypertext Markup Language (HTML)—the language used to create documents for the World Wide Web—has sent legions of would-be do-it-yourselfers in search of a pricey Internet consultant. For many, even the allegedly simplified manuals available in bookstores prove impenetrable. Worthy Internet-based projects get shelved, done in by high costs or technophobia.

But Means insists that learning HTML is really not such a difficult task. In fact, he spent all of a week teaching himself enough of the computer coding to build and run his Web site. Add to that about

$50 worth of off-the-shelf software and $26 a month for an America Online account, and the Public Access Project's voice had joined the burgeoning online chorus.

Means makes no apologies for his liberal point of view, but he works hard to keep the Public Access Project site free of anything that he believes readers may deem propaganda. "I want to be a librarian and a publisher, rather than a polemicist," he says.

Instead, the home page serves up hefty doses of raw data that he and others have culled from government files—legislators' financial-disclosure forms, for example, or a rundown of Chicago scofflaws. A subset of that parking-violators list happens to include public officials and public employees—comprehensive lists that the Windy City's daily papers have never published but that Means thinks will be instructive for voters or candidates looking for the lowdown on their rivals.

Public Access sometimes analyzes data as well. The group examined the campaign contributions of Illinois casino and racetrack owners, for example, and revealed trends in whose favors were being curried. Another study tracks the financing of judicial campaigns, an area of particular local interest given Chicago's rich history of judges selling verdicts. But the group's nonprofit status prohibits it from reaching conclusions about the in-office performance or the fitness for office of incumbents or challengers. Rather, Public Access merely exposes relevant information for the electorate's judgment.

To safeguard against charges of bias, Means posts all his study data on the Web site—a strategy he recommends to others. The reason: Others have an opportunity to rerun the numbers and to check his methodology. "It's easy to give my opinions credibility," he says, "because I'll show you how I reached this conclusion and you can use the same data to reach different conclusions.

"Using the Web can be far more than a personal platform. You can educate and show that your resources have credibility."

Ultimately, Means says, the job of an organization like his is merely to lay out the data for public scrutiny, to expose the money chase. "Let's let people know how government works and who it works for," he adds. "If they think it's a bad situation, they can change it."

This approach has made the Public Access Project's Web site particularly popular among journalists and political activists, who are handed the facts and figures without any accompanying spin. Also of use to Web-site visitors are the accompanying hyperlinks to a wide variety of information about local, state, and national political issues. There is the complete list of lobbyists registered with the Illinois Secretary of State, for example, and the full text of a General Accounting Office study that shows the state's poor performance in redressing school funding inequities between poor and wealthy districts. There are links to government agencies, nonprofit organizations, and resources for those interested in the intricacies of FOIA. And there are comprehensive lists of publicly accessible records for various state, county, and city agencies—detailed blueprints that can assist would-be muckrakers in identifying documents, newsletters, and brochures they might otherwise be unaware of. These include everything from daily employee time reports and internal memoranda to payroll sheets, housing-inspection checklists, and ethics-disclosure filings. It also includes contacts for computer-generated records.

Means is compiling these lists via a FOIA request to every agency. It's an enormous undertaking, and one that ultimately will remove historical barriers to disclosure of government documents. "If you contact the Chicago Department of Aviation and ask for a budget, they may tell you they don't have such a document," Means explains. "The problem is that you haven't called it by the right name, so they don't have to give it to you. But if I publish a list of what they compile, I give people a roadmap of what to ask for." As a bonus, he says, the agency will be encouraged to publish the documents, and he can simply link to its Web site from the Public Access home page.

In addition, the site maintains online versions of *Public Access News*, the organization's newsletter. Using an automated phone distribution list, Means faxes the publication to opinion-makers, board members, contributors, and other interested parties. It's nothing fancy—just a two-column, stock-format newsletter composed in Microsoft Word. But it encapsulates the key information and findings, making for a quick and valuable read.

But it's the Web site that really sets the Public Access Project apart. Means hopes to expand its online offerings, although doing so would require a heftier budget. He would also like to see his home page replicated by like-minded activists in other jurisdictions. That, he says, would help people know how government works and whom it works for. And it would, he notes, add more critical voices to this electronic "citizens' megaphone."

Venturing into Cyberspace

So you want to build a Web site? Join the world's fastest-growing club.

Broadcasting digital messages to the masses has proved to be a powerful lure for organizations, corporations, and individuals. But as many can testify, there's more to building a home page than simply throwing a few documents online. There are, in fact, many decisions facing first-timers, not the least of which is how to find an Internet service provider. There are commercial providers that cater to non-profits, but the fine print of some of their contracts may leave you longing for the mimeograph machine. Jayne Cravens, whose consulting firm, Coyote Communications (www.coyotecom.com), has ushered many nonprofits onto the Net, has some sound advice regarding the selection of a Web space provider:

She notes, for example, that a lot of groups offer free services for six months, giving clients time to promote their new sites and to generate traffic. But the free service gives way to very steep charges, forcing organizations to make an unhappy choice: pay the inflated costs or else take down the site and remove the Internet address from the letterhead, newsletter, and so on.

That's not to say there aren't good free Web-site providers, adds Cravens. But before contracting with one, she recommends that you ask these questions:

- What are your rates after the first six months (or whatever the time period) of free service?

- Would you charge for links from our Web site to other sites or to an e-mail address?

- Would you allow cgi scripts on my site? (A cgi script—short for common gateway interface—is a mechanism that permits viewers to enter information, such as surveys, that's returned to the Web server for processing.) Would you charge for cgi scripts on my site?

- What would the domain name of our Web site be? Do you offer the nonprofit its own domain name? Having a domain name may not be important to your nonprofit, but you definitely don't want a Web site with an address that you can't remember and recite off the top of your head.

- How easy will it be for me to change information on our site? Can I do it from my own computer, or do I have to provide the information to someone at your organization? If the latter is true, how long will it take for information to be changed once I provide it to you?

- What are the names and Web addresses for some of your long-term clients?

- If I eventually move my Web site somewhere else, will you keep a link to my new site on the page where my home page used to be? If so, for how long?

If you don't like the answers you get, says Cravens, or if you don't understand them, don't do business with a free Web-site provider.

As for tracking down low-cost providers, try this address: www.budgetweb.com/lowcost. You'll find information on low-cost Internet providers who will host your home page, along with graphic designers and scanning services to help you improve it.

Freeloading

The hourly fees to search some databases are enough to make you run to old standbys like *The Reader's Guide to Periodical Literature*. Fortunately, an increasing number of libraries now offer patrons no-cost searches, and there are also numerous Internet-accessible databases that can be searched for free.

Anyone with access to the Library of Congress, in Washington, D.C., for example, may tap into Books in Print, Dissertation Abstracts, a database of Internet resources, an index of articles from more than 12,000 journals, and DataTimes, which indexes stories from regional newspapers. EventLine will help you find schedules for conventions and exhibits worldwide, while PapersFirst is a database of papers presented at conferences. Another useful online tool at the library is InfoTrac, which provides articles about companies, their subsidiaries, and related industries.

Many libraries offer CD-ROM collections. Look for *Business Dataline*, which includes such resources as a full-text index to business newsletters as well as seemingly endless information about small companies. Also be aware that many reference books may also be available online and/or on CD-ROM, both of which provide more powerful search options. For example, the *Encyclopedia of Business Information Sources* (Gale)—which includes everything from databases and trade associations to research centers, professional societies, and annual directories—is also published on CD-ROM.

There are valuable reference works available that will help you find databases of interest. Two more published by Gale are particularly helpful: *The Federal Database Finder* lists free and fee-based databases and files available from the federal government, while the *Directory of Databases* covers commercially available databases.

Yet another Gale directory worth exploring is *The CyberHound's Guide to Internet Databases*, an annual volume that includes a subject index to new databases.

Internet search engines will also help you find your way to no-cost databases. Here are some that may be useful:

- If you're searching out news about a company, its own press releases are worth tracking down. One easy way is via PR Newswire, which lets you search for news by industry, company, stock symbol, or state, as well as by key words. The address is www.prnewswire.com.

- Most major newspapers and other large media organizations have Web sites where you can search for news stories that they have carried. But many do impose fees, especially for items that aren't current. The Chico (California) High School Library has a large set of links to various news archives: <u>dewey.chs.chico.k12.ca.us /news-ss.html</u>.

- If you're looking for the full-text version of past and pending federal legislation back to 1973, committee reports back to 1995, or *The Congressional Record* back to 1990, it's all available on Thomas, an online service of the Library of Congress: <u>thomas.loc.gov</u>.

- *Who's Who* can be a valuable source of information about people of interest. It's there for the searching—phone numbers included—at: <u>www.whoswho-online.com/search.html</u>.

- If you find a phone number in your notes but can't remember whom it belongs to, try the free Reverse Look-up at: **www.555-1212.com/look_up.cfm**.

Low Tech, High Yield

Like many public libraries, Washington, D.C.'s Martin Luther King, Jr., Memorial Library installed some high-tech search equipment in recent years. On the ground floor, for example, researchers have access to computers with CD-ROM drives that offer full-text health information and citations to newspaper and magazine articles from hundreds of publications. The wealth of information served up on these computer terminals—and the ease of retrieving it—makes them popular. As a result, patrons can expect to wait.

But two floors up, in the library's Washingtoniana Division, there's a valuable storehouse of information that few ever take advantage of: the clip files of the defunct *Washington Star*. Maybe it's the mustiness of the old, yellowed paper that keeps people away. Or maybe researchers don't like having to unfold clips and place them on the photocopier. Or maybe they simply don't know the collection exists.

Whatever the reason, savvy muckrakers realize that relying only on the latest research tools will not always get them the whole story. Although thousands of publications can be searched online, archival materials are generally not available. Good luck trying to track down ten- or twenty-year-old stories from major newspapers online. In fact, it's hard to find five years' worth for many publications. In short, when searching for information, don't automatically assume that everything will be available on CD-ROM or the Internet. Instead, map out a strategy that exploits all media, including newspaper clip files (assuming you can gain access), a library or company's vertical files, microfilm, microfiche, and so on.

Here are some widely available resources that will help you track down special-interest information:

- **Guide to Microforms in Print.** Published by K.G. Saur, this volume includes all newspapers, dates for which microfilm is available, and vendors.

- **Books in Print.** They may be low-tech, but there's no shortage of reference books listed in it that will likely be of use. Published by R.R. Bowker, this annual, multi-volume set includes a valuable subject guide.

- **Directories in Print.** An annual volume published by Gale, it includes contents, cost, and ordering information.

- **The Serials Directory.** EBSCO Publishing's comprehensive listing of newspapers and other serials.

- **Newsletters in Print.** Like other Gale publications, the data in this directory is also available on CD-ROM and through various online search services, including Lexis-Nexis.

Web Sights (and Sounds)

Building a page on the World Wide Web is not technically difficult, but designing an engaging and useful one is another matter. While many sites dazzle visitors with their graphics, interactive features, and wealth of information, others are obvious candidates to be condemned. Most fall somewhere in between.

If you're going to make the leap, there's no reason to reinvent the cyberwheel. Instead, learn from those who have already been there and done that. Here are eight Web sites built by muckrakers, magazines, and advocacy organizations with features worth emulating.

- **FECInfo,** www.tray.com/fecinfo

  It isn't flashy, but Tony Raymond's Web site is crammed with valuable information about federal candidates, and it's laid out in a way that makes it easy to use. Raymond was an eighteen-year veteran of the Federal Election Commission before he left to consult on—what else?—election-related matters. FECInfo is an impressive compilation of databases that run the gamut from political action committees and campaign-contributor occupations to the zip codes from which the most campaign dollars flow. Type "Trump" in one database, for example, and immediately see to whom the well-known casino owner (and others with this surname) handed money last election cycle. In addition, various huge databases may be downloaded for off-line scrutiny.

- **20/20 Vision,** www.2020vision.org

  20/20 Vision is a Washington, D.C.-based nonprofit advocacy organization whose focus is protecting the environment and promoting peace through grassroots action. After paying the annual membership dues, each month members are sent a postcard identifying the best way to spend 20 minutes trying to advance the group's goals. The Web site augments the organization's efforts by posting the monthly action alerts, which provide detailed information about the problem and where to call or write to voice concern. The site also includes a useful section called "Tools for Activism"—a series of documents that teach readers effective ways to reach policymakers, to craft op-ed pieces, and so on.

- **Mother Jones Magazine,** www.mojones.com/mother_jones

  The well-known magazine of investigative reporting makes articles from its current issue available over a two-month period, while more than six years' worth are available in their entirety. (A search engine lets readers fish out articles of interest from this archive.) Those so inclined can join in various online discussions; those so impressed can subscribe online.

- **Corporate Watch,** www.corpwatch.org

  The cosponsor of the Greenwash Award, which singles out environmentally unfriendly corporations that pose as do-gooders, Corporate Watch has a beautifully designed Web site that features this dubious achievement and invites reader nominations. Among the site's many other features are a comprehensive guide to researching transnational corporations, a letters-to-the-editor section that reprints representative e-mail, and sign-up instructions for the group's "listserv," a special-interest mailing list that sends subscribers announcements and alerts. Also featured are excerpts from a book authored by a Corporate Watch staff member, complete with an online form to purchase the volume with a credit card.

- **Join Together Online,** www.jointogether.org

  A national resource for communities working to reduce substance abuse and gun violence, the organization's Web site includes such features as current news articles, a resource center with more than a thousand relevant articles, and a searchable database of over 70,000 people across the nation working on substance abuse. Another noteworthy feature is an events calendar that can be searched by key word, organization, date, and so on. What's more, groups may add their own events to the calendar while online.

- **Environmental Working Group,** www.ewg.org

  The nonprofit environmental research and policy-analysis organization, which is a project of a large foundation, maintains an easy-to-navigate Web site that offers prominence to its investigative reports, which may be downloaded in their entirety. In addition, the site maintains a variety of databases that allow users to explore issues specific to their communities. For example, click on a state and you're brought to a menu that includes such subjects as violations of federal tap-water standards and wetlands-destruction permits issued by the U.S. Army Corps of Engineers. Click on the latter and you find a decade's worth of permits, details of which are available farther down the menu. It's a good example of turning large amounts of national data into a format that makes it of purely local interest.

- **Transactional Records Access Clearinghouse,** www.trac.syr.edu

  TRAC is a data-gathering, -research, and -distribution organization associated with Syracuse University. Established in 1989, its purpose is to provide comprehensive information about the activities of federal enforcement and regulatory agencies, as well as the communities in which they take place. To that end, a massive amount of federal agency data obtained through Freedom of Information Act requests is checked and verified, then mounted on the Web site. This is a plain-vanilla home page that exists to make available important information, not to wow Web surfers with bells and whistles.

- **McSpotlight,** www.envirolink.org/mcspotlight/home.html

  In 1990, two activists involved with London Greenpeace were sued for allegedly distributing a six-sided fact sheet criticizing McDonald's. The trial, which gave all indications of never ending, generated much worldwide interest, as the two defendants decided to defend themselves in court. The Web site they built to chronicle the trial—and to help raise funds for their defense—offers a soup-to-nuts compilation of everything with any kind of relevance. There are press backgrounders, debate rooms, and an avalanche of legal documents that include some 30,000 pages of court transcripts gathered over three days. There is also a narrated tour of the site using Real Audio technology. And there's a tour of McDonald's Web site that's annotated with the defendants' version of the corporation's practices.

Just the Facts, Please

Some mistakes can have life-or-death consequences.

For example, a *Newsweek* special edition on "Your Child" recommended that five-month-olds be allowed to feed themselves zwiebacks and raw carrot chunks. But when a pediatrician informed the editors that babies that young can choke on hard foods, hundreds of thousands of copies were recalled. The mistake was corrected and the issue reprinted.

Most print errors don't carry such grievous consequences, but fact-checking should nonetheless be a routine step in the production of reports and studies. As many authors have discovered, errors—no matter how insignificant—can be used to question the veracity of the entire work. It is a common—and often effective—technique of a study's target to hold out even unimportant errors of fact as proof that the work's damaging conclusions should also be questioned. This tactic often diverts attention from the real issues, leaving a frustrated author on the defensive.

As a result, pay close attention to every fact, every figure, every quote. Here are some things to be aware of:

- Don't automatically assume that something you read in even the most respected publication is necessarily true. A name, date, job title, or affiliation in Monday's newspaper may be corrected in Tuesday's. Multiple sources can help protect against reprinting inaccuracies.

- Consider the source of the information you're using. If the publication is notorious for its extreme points of view, make certain that the data you're citing is rooted in fact, not mere opinion.

- Pay particular attention to the source of information that's downloaded from the Internet, where rumor and theory are often circulated as bible truth. Be particularly suspicious of anonymous and overly biased writings.

- Be aware that information culled from databases may not always be accurate. For example, information on licenses and permits often comes directly from the applicant, and therefore may not be entirely truthful. What's more, that handwritten information is typically then keyed into a database—another possibility for error. Try to determine if those records were fact-checked.

- Consider the author you're citing. Check to find out whether this person is an expert in the field, has published other articles or books on the same topic, or has journalistic credentials that would make her a credible source. Once again, pay close attention to the authorship of articles you find on the Web. If the writings are filled with grammatical mistakes and spelling errors, or if the claims seem wildly exaggerated, that should be a tip-off that the author's background needs to be investigated.

- Always pay attention to numbers. Recalculate your findings to make sure the math is correct. If you're using statistics, attach the raw numbers to your study so others can run their own calculations.

- Check quotes carefully. If you recorded interviews, keep copies of the tapes. If you put quotation marks around someone's words, be certain those are the exact words. Altering someone's words not only may damage your credibility but could also leave you vulnerable to a libel suit.

- Never publish an "anonymous tip"—be it via an out-of-the-blue phone call or a letter with no signature—without confirming the information. Once again, failure to do so could both ruin your credibility and bring you legal problems.

- When fact-checking your work, don't overlook anything. Check the spelling of middle names. Check dates. If you're reprinting photos, maps, or other artwork, check the sources. You don't want to learn after the fact that the photo you included of ABC Corporation's pollution-belching smokestack is actually a shot of another company's facilities.

- If you're reprinting copyrighted material not covered by fair use, make certain you've received permission *in writing*.

- If you've included footnotes in your document, check them carefully. Make certain you've cited the correct article, its publication date, and the page number.

- Be certain that your data is not outdated, particularly if you're citing scientific or technological information.

- All writing should be edited for grammar, spelling, and punctuation. What's more, pay close attention to consistency of facts. For example, if you claim in your executive summary that 350 fish are estimated to have been killed by a local factory's illegal chemical discharges, make certain that the text itself uses the same number.

CHAPTER TEN

Spreading the Message

After all the digging is done and the interviews completed, there remains one not-so-trivial matter: Will the world care about this investigation? Of course, there's an even more immediate question: Will the world ever even find out about it?

When all is said and done, some groups simply hand their materials to a reporter and hope for the best. Others call a press conference to announce their findings. Still others publish a study, post their findings on the Internet, or testify before a government committee.

No matter what method is used, the presentation must be professional: It should be accurate, well written, edited for style and substance, proofread, and polished. And, ultimately, it should be distributed to those inclined to help disseminate it.

Like other groups that seek to expose wrongdoing, the Center for Public Integrity has used a variety of means to make our work public, including reports, studies, and books. One powerful method has also been the newsletter—a concise, low-cost, easy-to-distribute format that has proved very effective. One issue of that newsletter, *The Public i*—entitled "Fat Cat Hotel"—reverberated well beyond the Beltway.

Excerpts from that edition of the newsletter follow. Since fall 1999, *The Public i* has been published online, at www.public-i.org. To see earlier issues, along with some of the Center's other investigative studies, visit our Web site at www.publicintegrity.org. Information is also available by writing the Center at: 910 17th Street, NW, Seventh Floor, Washington, D.C. 20006; (202) 466-1300.

From "Fat Cat Hotel"

In June 1996, *Forbes* magazine reported that the Democratic National Committee was using overnight stays at the White House as a perk to entice wealthy donors to make six-figure contributions to the party. For a contribution of $130,000, "you can spend the night in Abraham Lincoln's bed," ABC News' David Brinkley, picking up on the *Forbes* item, said on *This Week with David Brinkley*, the Sunday-morning television show. "But be warned. I am told Lincoln's bed is hard and lumpy."

"This has become an urban myth, like the alligators in the sewers of New York," Amy Weiss Tobe, the DNC's press secretary, told the Center for Public Integrity. "It is just not true."

There's nothing unusual, of course, about politicians and political parties "servicing" their donors and fund-raisers. In the summer of 1995, the DNC—in a letter signed by the party's co-chairmen, Senator Christopher Dodd of Connecticut and Donald Fowler, and first disclosed by the *Chicago Sun-Times*—offered potential supporters a "menu" of rewards. A contribution of $100,000 or more, for example, would get a donor two meals with President Clinton, two meals with Vice President Albert Gore, Jr., a slot on a foreign trade mission with DNC leaders, and other benefits, such as a daily fax report and an assigned DNC staff member to assist with the donor's "personal requests."

Fowler responded to charges that the party and the President were selling access and influence to contributors by saying that such fund-raising efforts would continue until the law requires both parties to operate differently. "Until the system is changed, we will not unilaterally disarm," Fowler reportedly said, accurately reflecting the fact that every party and administration has given special treatment to its biggest supporters. A Democratic lobbyist familiar with perks for contributors told *National Journal* that spending the night at the White House was like having access to "the best candy store in town."

The Center for Public Integrity has determined that, since 1993, more than 75 Democratic contributors and fund-raisers have spent the night in the White House—mostly in the Lincoln or Queen's Bedroom—as guests of President and Mrs. Clinton.

When guests spend the night in the Lincoln or the Queen's Bedroom, they receive five-star treatment. At night, the beds are turned down and breakfast menus placed on the beds. Guests may choose where they would like to eat breakfast—possibly in the solarium or the sitting room next to the Lincoln Bedroom—and which newspapers they would like to read in the morning. Most guests receive a pass to roam the White House's residential quarters. Almost every guest with whom the Center for Public Integrity spoke said that spending the night in the White House was an honor.

It is important to note that not all of the overnight guests at the White House are contributors or fund-raisers. Ann Lewis, the Clinton campaign's deputy manager and director of communications, sent a letter to Brinkley in which she pointed out that many others have slept in the Lincoln Bedroom, including "the cook from Clinton's old governor's mansion in Little Rock, a theology student with his wife and two children, and an old friend who is not well, and the president's pastor and his wife, and none of them paid as much as a dime," Brinkley said on the following week's program. Other overnight guests have included former President George Bush; former President and Mrs. Jimmy Carter; Leah Rabin, the widow of Yitzak Rabin, the late Israeli Prime Minister; former Texas Governor Ann Richards; and Lee Iacocca, the former chairman and chief executive officer of Chrysler Corporation.

The Democratic fat cats who've spent the night at the White House include Steven Grossman, the president of Massachusetts Envelope Company, and his wife, Barbara. They attended a state dinner for the president of Brazil in April 1995 and, later that evening, retired to the historic Queen's Bedroom. Steven Grossman told the Center that it was "a memorable evening" and that he was "honored" to have been invited to the White House. When asked what he thought about Brinkley's report on sleepovers at the White House for substantial contributions to the Democratic Party, Grossman replied, "I have no comment."

The Grossmans have contributed at least $400,000 to the Democratic Party and to Clinton since 1991. In 1994, Clinton appointed Barbara Grossman, who is a professor of theater at Tufts University, to the National Council for the Arts. Steven Grossman is the president of the American Israel Public Affairs Committee and has been a managing trustee of the DNC. Grossman, a former chairman of the Massachusetts Democratic Party, told the Center for Public Integrity that he has "a working relationship" with President Clinton that goes back many years.

Another Democratic contributor whom President Clinton invited to spend the night at the White House was Lew Wasserman, the former chairman of MCA, Inc., an entertainment conglomerate. Although Wasserman has spent the night in the White House at the invitation of various presidents, his clout within the Democratic Party has given him special access to Democratic Presidents.

In the late 1970s, the late John White, then the chairman of the Democratic National Committee, informed Wasserman that the Democratic Party might have to vacate its Washington headquarters because of a financial shortfall brought on by the multimillion-dollar debt from the 1968 presidential campaign. Wasserman proceeded to take out his checkbook and write a substantial check that kept the DNC offices open, White told the Center in a 1993 interview.

What did Wasserman seek in return? Not anything, really, White told the Center. But there was one occasion, he recalled, when Wasserman was coming to Washington and couldn't find a hotel room. He called White, who telephoned the owner of Washington's expensive Madison Hotel, imploring him to accommodate Mr. Wasserman. Unfortunately, no room was available. White smiled proudly and recalled that he finally found overnight lodging for the wealthy Hollywood mogul—at the White House, in the Lincoln Bedroom. This favor for Wasserman, White said, was "just a small thing."

Wasserman and his wife, Edie, have spent the night in the Lincoln Bedroom at least twice during the Clinton presidency and have contributed at least $450,000 to Clinton and the Democratic Party since 1991. He has also contributed to Clinton's Legal Expense Trust, established by the President and Mrs. Clinton to help pay for their mounting legal bills from the Whitewater investigation and the Paula Jones sexual-harassment lawsuit. In 1992, Wasserman invited 100 of his friends to attend a fund-raiser for Clinton and the Democratic Party sponsored by the Hollywood Women's Political Committee. The minimum price of admission: $5,000. In June 1996, Wasserman hosted a fund-raiser that raised more than $1 million for the Democratic Party. Over the years, Wasserman has contributed more than $1 million to the Democrats. He declined the Center's request for an interview.

Included here was a partial list of Democratic contributors and fund-raisers who had spent the night at the Clinton White House since 1993. Accompanying that list was the following sidebar:

Top Secret

The names of overnight guests at the Clinton White House are a closely guarded secret.

"This is their [the First Family's] home, and they have guests visit them all the time," Neel Lattimore, Mrs. Clinton's press secretary, told the Center for Public Integrity. "Mrs. Clinton and Chelsea have friends that spend the night, but these names are not available to the public."

Friends of Mrs. Clinton and Chelsea, however, aren't the only guests who spend the night at the White House. The Center for Public Integrity determined that many Democratic contributors and fund-raisers have been invited to spend the night at the White House. Over the past few months, the Center asked White House officials for a list of all guests who have stayed overnight at the White House at the invitation of President and Mrs. Clinton, but they repeatedly side-stepped all inquiries, referring the Center to other offices.

The Center asked George Stephanopoulos, a senior adviser to President Clinton, whether he knew of Democratic contributors who had been invited to stay in the Lincoln Bedroom. "I don't know any-thing about that," Stephanopoulos said, directing the Center to the White House Social Secretary's office.

"I don't think there is a list like that," Heather Raiden of the Social Secretary's office told the Center. "No one in the White House will release that kind of information about guests anyway. I think it's for security reasons."

The Center for Public Integrity sent Freedom of Information Act requests to the counsel to the President and to the Secret Service. "The Office of the President, including the President's immediate personal staff and units within the Executive Office whose sole function is to advise and assist the President, is not an 'agency' for purposes of FOIA," Marvin Krislov, an associate counsel to the President, replied in a letter. "Consequently, FOIA does not establish a statutory right to the documents that you have requested from the Office of the President, if such documents exist."

The Center sent a follow-up letter to Krislov, pointing out that the White House could voluntarily provide the documents even if FOIA did not apply. He did not reply to the letter, nor did he return subsequent telephone calls from the Center. Krislov resigned from the White House on March 31, 1996, to become the Labor Department's deputy solicitor for national operations. John Simpson, the Secret Service's Freedom of Information and Privacy Acts officer, said that the Secret Service doesn't "have a list like that and we wouldn't break it down like that...who stayed in what rooms and who stayed overnight."

The Center determined that the Office of the Usher at the White House is the custodian of records that include overnight guests. "These records are for private use by the First Family," said Dennis Freemyer, an assistant usher who has worked in the White House for four administrations. "They have always been used that way for every President, and we do not divulge information to the public or press about these records."

The usher's logbook records the movements of the President, First Lady, and others in the family quarters at the White House, including the hour the President gets up in the morning, eats dinner at night, who visits the residential quarters, and which rooms guests stay in. Such logbooks have been maintained for more than 100 years and reflect the comings and goings in the residential quarters of the White House. At the end of a presidential term, when the First Family leaves the White House, the logbooks are presented to the First Lady.

As White House records go, the usher's logbooks are clearly one of the best-kept secrets. "I worked in the Carter Library for ten years before I came to work on the Bush project, and I can tell you I have never heard of these records and I have never seen them," David Alsobrook, the acting director of the Bush Presidential Materials Project, told the Center. Nor have the archivists working with presidential papers at the National Archives and at the Reagan and Carter libraries heard of them.

The reason that archivists, and many other experts the Center talked to, have never heard of the logbooks is that Presidents have typically categorized them as personal records. The Presidential Records Act of 1978 draws a distinction between "Presidential records" and "personal records," noting that the government "shall reserve and retain complete ownership, possession, and control of the Presidential records."

The law defines personal records as "all documentary materials... of a purely private or nonpublic character which do not relate to or have an effect upon the carrying out of the constitutional, statutory, or other official or ceremonial duties of the President."

Who decides which records are "Presidential" and which are "personal"? The President. "The act says that the incumbent president and his staff decide what are personal records and what are presidential records," Nancy Smith, an archivist at the National Archives, said. The applicable portion of the law reads as follows: "Documentary materials produced or received by the President, his staff, or units or individuals in the Executive Office of the President...shall, to the extent practicable, be categorized as Presidential records or personal records upon their creation or receipt and be filed separately."

The line between personal activities and "constitutional, statutory, or other official or ceremonial duties of the President" seems to be blurry since government officials and foreign dignitaries, to name a few, often visit the President on official business in the First Family's residential quarters.

Although President Lyndon B. Johnson donated his logbooks to the LBJ Library in Austin, Texas, the records were considered to be part of Johnson's most confidential papers and only became open to the public in 1993.

In 1974, Patricia Nixon did away with the logbooks because she felt that they "were too personal—what time they get up, what they eat for breakfast, the names of their friends coming in," according to a 1974 column in *The Washington Post*.

For Immediate Release

If you want to make news, learn to write a good news release.

Media outlets are bombarded with press releases, many of which go straight to the recycling bin without being read. But this form of communication is nonetheless the way business is done—it's the means by which reporters get many of their story leads. As a result, you need to learn the right way to craft a release. Otherwise, the report that took your organization months to compile—no matter how newsworthy—may be relegated to that same recycling pile.

So consider what's right and wrong about the sample news release on the next page.

"For Immediate Release" tells a reporter that the materials may be used immediately, that there is no "embargo" date.

There is no date at the top of the release, as there should be.

Both home and office phone numbers are a good idea, because you want reporters to be able to reach you on deadline with questions. Ditto for the e-mail address.

An attention-getting headline—centered, as it should be—is indeed likely to get a reporter's attention. But an attention-getting headline with a misspelled "Diesel"—an element central to the story—will immediately call into question your credibility. Remember: Proofread everything.

The dateline tells the reporter "where" and is therefore a good idea.

CITIZEN MUCKRAKING

CITIZENS FOR ENVIRONMENTAL EQUILIBRIUM

1711 Rubar Road
Teaneck, NJ 07666
Tel: (201) 555-7649
Fax: (201) 555-5424

FOR IMMEDIATE RELEASE
CONTACT: Mitchell Pitkin
(201) 555-7649 (office)
(201) 555-1882 (home)
mitchpit@noarena.org

STUDY REVEALS THAT PROPOSED DEASEL REFURBISHING PLANT MAY IMPERIL TOWN'S DRINKING WATER

(Teaneck, NJ) — A six-month study released today concludes that the city's water supply may be severely compromised by construction of the diesel-engine refurbishing plant now under consideration by the city council. "Hidden Dangers," which was authored by members of the grassroots organization Citizens for Environmental Equilibrium, concludes that the runoff of solvents from the facility would contaminate groundwater and jeopardize the public health.

Among the other key findings of the gripping and provocative 58-page report:

- The city's environmental-impact statement does not address storm-water pollution, as required by the federal Environmental Protection Agency.

- Independent experts maintain that consultants to the city underestimated the impact the proposed plant would have on the town's lucrative rockfish and oyster fisheries.

- The facility's contractor, who, documents reveal, was formerly married to the city-council president's sister, has twice been convicted of bid rigging and ten years ago lost his construction license after admitting to illegally dumping toxic chemicals near the Hackensack Reservoir.

"The evidence is overwhelming," said Rory Flynn, president of Citizens for Environmental Equilibrium. "This factory is likely to have devastating health consequences for Teaneck residents."

Citizens for Environmental Equilibrium is a nonprofit, educational organization that has been granted 501(c)(3) status by the Internal Revenue Service. Copies of "Hidden Dangers" are available to the media and others for $5 per copy.

☺ ☺ ☺

As soon as possible—i.e., in the first paragraph—you also want to tell the reporter who, what, and when.

This text is mostly simple and factual—a good model for your news releases.

But leave the editorializing and hyperbole (gripping and provocative) out of it.

If possible, keep the news release to one 8-1/2 x 11 page. White paper is fine. Leave substantial margins. And always double-space the type to keep it readable.

Journalists talk about "burying the lede"—that is, inadvertently putting the most provocative piece of information far down in the story instead of at the beginning. If you've got a blockbuster finding, make sure to highlight it near the top so no one will miss it.

A (not-long-winded) quote from an organization official is good form.

Background about the organization will help identify it for those reporters unfamiliar with your work.

The report may be available for sale to the public, but there's no charge to reporters (the people giving you all that free publicity). A copy of the report should be sent with the news release.

You may be happy that someone actually read your release to the end, but save the smiley faces for your kid's lunchbox. A press release should end with a standard journalistic convention, which is centered:

—30—

Behind the Newsroom Door

Suppose you held a press conference and nobody came. It's an unnerving prospect, but take heart: You'd have plenty of company.

Many groups have suffered the indignity of releasing their work to no one but their members. They may blame the media for ignoring an important story, but they should instead blame themselves for not taking steps to ensure that reporters pay attention.

Even if you write a first-class news release, it's of no value if it doesn't find its way to the proper people. Furthermore, it had better arrive there at the right time—that is, well before deadline. Sending your report about zoning-department malfeasance to the guy who covers Little League is not likely to get you on page one. And calling radio stations that air only syndicated national news reports will not be a good use of your time.

There are no hard and fast rules about dealing with the media, because operating procedures may change from one medium to another, or even from one outlet to the next. For example, while large radio stations typically have a definite hierarchy, a small radio station may have a single person who's a reporter in the morning, an editor in the afternoon, and an on-air interviewer at day's end. Similarly, reporters at a small-town weekly will probably have different responsibilities than do their counterparts at big-city dailies: The former are invariably generalists who cover everything, while the latter may be assigned "beats"—they focus on an issue or area of interest.

There is no need to know everyone involved with a news operation, but there is a small cadre who can get exposure for your muckraking efforts. These include:

- **Assignment editor.** This is the person who decides what's news— or at least what's worthy of coverage. The flow of news releases and wire-service stories end up with the assignment editor, who then marshals the reporters, photographers, and other editorial troops. You're not likely to have personal contact with an assignment editor, as this is a behind-the-scenes job. But when all else fails, addressing a news release to the attention of an assignment editor may prove useful.

- **Producer.** In TV Land, the producer pulls some heavy strings. If a local broadcaster regularly airs a consumer or environmental report, for instance, those segments are likely to have their own producers. Making contact with such producers can pay dividends, because they usually have a say in what airs.

- **Daybook editor.** Reporters learn of speeches, news conferences, and other events via "daybooks" of major wire services like United Press International and the Associated Press. In addition, some smaller, regional news services also compile these calendars of events. Phone, fax, or mail your information, along with a contact name and phone number, to the local daybook editor at least two days before the event. Call the day before to make certain the information has been received.

- **Reporter.** Reporters are always eager for a good story. They arrive at their desks each day worried that they'll have nothing to cover, that the competition will "scoop" them. Most reporters are therefore eager for story ideas and welcome being tipped off to something noteworthy. Therefore, if your group is working on an investigative effort that's likely to produce news, make contact with a reporter in advance of releasing your findings. Study a publication or newscast to determine which reporter covers pertinent issues. If possible, give a reporter ample time to understand the nature of your investigation and to digest data you may have unearthed—particularly if it's complicated material. That may mean sharing pieces of the story along the way—but only with the understanding that the findings may not be published until you say so. It may also mean "leaking" an exclusive to a reporter or giving journalists an advance copy of your study with an "embargo" date for publication.

Don't aim only for the biggest media outlets. If you have a story that may legitimately interest national media, by all means pitch it there. But develop a comprehensive list of all appropriate outlets. That means local newspapers and broadcasters. It may also mean magazines, special-interest newsletters, trade publications, community newspapers, and the like.

There are a number of directories, available in many libraries, that will help you identify contacts at local and national media outlets. These include:

- **Bacon's *TV/Cable Directory*.** Lists programming contacts, news directors, and assignment editors at TV stations and cable channels.

- **Bacon's *Radio Directory*.** A companion volume that lists radio-station news contacts.

- ***Broadcasting & Cable Yearbook*.** Published by R.R. Bowker, this annual volume includes addresses, phone numbers, and names of broadcast news directors.

- ***Editor & Publisher Yearbook*.** Details newspaper personnel, including wire services.

Opportunity Knocks

A decade ago, making news was a formulaic affair: Throw a press conference, and they will come. Serve coffee and cake, and they will be there on time.

That's no longer the case, although the news conference has by no means gone the way of the electric typewriter. A news conference is a convenient way to release a bona fide news story. After all, it permits you to make whistleblowers or nationally recognized experts available for interviews; it also lets you preview undercover video, hand out recently declassified documents, or go on location downstream from where a factory has been found to be illegally dumping effluents.

If you decide to stage a press conference, find a good public-relations guide that will lay out the generally accepted dos and don'ts, including:

- Keep the event to an hour.
- Stage it between 10 a.m. and 2 p.m.
- Hand out copies of prepared statements and background materials.

- Provide five to seven days' notice to reporters.

- Anticipate the special needs of the camera- and microphone-wielding broadcast media.

- Don't overlook this one: Provide both decaf and regular along with the cake.

But if a news conference only produces a story that can be told just as well with a press release, opt for the latter. Remember, don't squander your credibility by summoning reporters to a non-event, because they may stay away the next time when you have something truly newsworthy.

Also, explore ways of taking your story directly to the public. Consider these options:

- **Letters to the editor.** Surveys show that a newspaper's letters section is well read. Here's an opportunity to craft a concise summary of your findings or to issue a rebuttal to a point of view expressed in the paper.

- **Op-ed pieces.** The page facing a newspaper's editorial page offers an ideal forum to make a case for the work your group is doing. Contact the paper's editorial-page editor for guidelines on how to submit such a piece.

- **Talk shows.** Geraldo and Oprah may not want you as a guest, but the local radio or TV station that hosts a weekly public-affairs show might. Contact the host or producer with a letter detailing your work and the importance of the issue to the community at large.

In addition, consider some less traditional means of generating interest for your work—i.e., look to technological means of alerting the world. For example:

- Fax updates to the media and public-interest groups that may be interested in your work.

- If you have Internet access, Usenet is a set of special-interest "newsgroups." You can "post" articles or messages to Usenet groups whose readers may want to know about your work, findings, law-suits, and so on.

- There are thousands of special-interest mailing lists on the Internet, the most common of which are called "listservs." Messages sent to these mailing lists are in turn e-mailed to the entire list of subscribers. Therefore, if you're engaged in an environmental battle, for example, brief messages or queries can be e-mailed to appropriate listservs. There are searchable master lists on the World Wide Web, including one called Liszt, where you'll find more than 90,000 entries. The address is: www.liszt.com.

Strategies and Tactics

In football, the conventional wisdom is that a good defense is the best offense. In the muckraking business, a good offense is often the best defense.

At least that's the advice of some public-relations practitioners who are called on to defuse the situation following a muckraker's revelations. While the strategy of those criticized used to be to issue a "no comment" and lie low until the story is (hopefully) yesterday's news, aggressive countermeasures are now more in vogue. Instead of idly suffering the slings of negative news, those under attack these days aren't so passive.

That's important to remember, because the subject of your investigation—no matter how solid your facts or startling your revelations—may try to deflect the issue, call into question your conclusions, or even impugn your reputation. So be aware that even a front-page story can blow up in your face if the focus is artfully redirected.

To understand how the opposition may try to pull this off, consider the advice of Robert Dilenschneider, a well-known PR maven and the author of highly regarded industry handbooks. Not long ago, he spoke to his peers of a "new age of muckraking" and implored them in a speech to deal immediately with any crisis but to not overreact. "A crisis isn't a crisis unless people treat it like one," he said.

Spreading the Message

Here are eight critical guidelines Dilenschneider outlined for managing and diffusing "muckraking attacks":

- Make sure you have substance on your side. If you're positioning yourself as environmentally correct, make sure you can prove it.

- Assemble all the relevant data and then tell it all, tell it fast, and tell it through one source. The idea is to gain control over the story. When dealing with muckrakers, don't let them tell your story for you.

- Get a solution, even an interim one, as soon as possible. That solution can be as simple as "We are looking into the problem."

- Find a way to extend yourself to victims and their families.

- Thank as many people as possible who participated in the solution of the crisis.

- Involve your critics in the solution. "I call this strategy inviting the enemy in," Dilenschneider says. "With muckrakers, it's often useful to ask how they propose to solve the problem. That deflects them from attacking you to attacking the problem."

- Be a contrarian. If you're attacked with rhetoric, respond with substance. If you're attacked with substance, respond with rhetoric.

- After arriving at a solution, announce it without delay and declare that the crisis is behind you. "Often," Dilenschneider says, "the announcement becomes a self-fulfilling prophecy. Announcements properly issued can be powerful. To make them most effective, make sure that you have kept good lists during the crisis, including the phone and fax numbers of everyone in the loop, who should get the news as swiftly as possible."

Don't be surprised if the targets of your muckraking use such tactics in hopes of either turning the tables or walking away unscathed. Be prepared with some thank-yous, rhetoric, and, most important, substance of your own.

The Write Stuff

Imagine this: After months of digging through documents and interviewing informants, you prove that a local contractor has cut corners on the construction of a new elementary school. Not only have the shoddy—not to mention shady—practices brought the contractor pocketfuls of cash, but the well-being of the town's students, you discover, has also been seriously jeopardized.

The idea that this jerk has put children in harm's way infuriates you, so at the press conference to announce your group's investigation, you let loose: First you outline the findings, laying out for the media illegal cost-cutting measures, bribery of public officials, and other revelations that are meticulously documented. Then, for good measure, you let the press in on another little scoop: You have it on good authority that the bum was involved in some extramarital dalliances—with the building inspector, of all people—in the construction-site trailer.

This guy is "a sleazeball," you declare, then hurl a string of insults and graphic descriptions of him that are bleeped on the six-o'clock news.

The question is: Can you say those sorts of things about someone in public?

The answer is: Yes, you can, although there's something worth considering: Your actions might earn you a lawsuit.

Novice muckrakers (and even veterans) sometimes get themselves into hot water by failing to stay within the law, first in the collection of information (see page 136) and then in the dissemination. Free speech may be one of this nation's guiding constitutional provisions, but libelous speech isn't. Your organization's newsletter can voice a negative opinion about a local company, for example, but hurling insults at the CEO and falsely accusing him of certain practices or procedures could be grounds for a lawsuit.

Here, then, are some legal guidelines to consider when writing and distributing results of your investigative effort:

- **Fair is fair.** Including large, verbatim chunks of someone else's writing in your report or study is copyright infringement. However, you may paraphrase other works, and you may use government documents without leaving yourself vulnerable to legal action. Also, the "fair use" doctrine lets you copy a small part of an original work without violating copyright law. Unfortunately, there is no precise fair-use formula; using a few paragraphs of background from a book may constitute fair use, for example, but using that book's three most newsworthy paragraphs may not. Given such vagueness, the bottom line is: Use other people's words sparingly, paraphrase when possible, or seek an author's permission to quote from his or her work.

- **Liable for libel**. Writing something false about a person may call into question the veracity of your reporting, but it won't necessarily bring you legal trouble. However, publishing a false and "defamatory" statement about that person (that is, a statement that harms his or her reputation) may constitute grounds for libel. Libel is tricky. Laws vary from state to state, and various court cases make it difficult for non-lawyers to know if their statements are in fact actionable. For example, the Supreme Court ruled in a landmark 1964 case that a "public figure" could not sue for defamation without first showing that the publisher either knew its story was false or was "reckless" about the truth of what was published. Politicians and celebrities are considered by the courts to be public figures, but determining who else in a community is a public or private figure isn't always cut-and-dried. As a result, it's advisable to have sensitive or inflammatory materials reviewed by an attorney before you make them public. And in every instance be sure to check facts, confirm the accuracy of quotes, verify the backgrounds of sources before accepting their information as reliable, and try to get independent corroboration for any sensitive allegation.

- **Private parts**. You may know for certain that a shady contractor was pursuing extracurricular sexual activities in the job-site trailer, but making that information public may constitute an invasion of privacy. The test is whether publication of the story, no matter how truthful, is both offensive and not of legitimate public concern. Of course, if the building inspector is a party to the tryst, and the contractor is receiving special treatment, then such information may in fact be published without constituting an invasion of privacy. On the other hand, if the photographic evidence was obtained by illegally trespassing on the job site, then publishing it could be a problem. And one more caveat: If you instead learn of the affair from divorce records or other legally obtained public records, you're free to use that information in your document. In short, the laws that govern invasion of privacy can be as murky as libel laws, which means special attention must be paid to them.

Because these laws are confusing, always submit controversial material to an attorney for an advance review. For a better notion about what sorts of writing might get you in trouble, consider these two sources of information:

- **The Student Press Law Center**. Although this organization assists student journalists, its publications are of value to all. Some of these materials are general in nature, but others focus on specific areas that may be of value—topics such as access to campus crime statistics, college foundation records, faculty and school-employee personnel evaluations, and school-employee disciplinary records. The Center may be contacted at: 1815 N. Ft. Meyer Drive, Suite 900, Arlington, VA 22209; (703) 807-1904. In addition, the organization's Web site includes the online Legal Clinic, which offers comprehensive information on libel, copyright, and other media law topics. Some of the Center's publications are available for free on the site as well. The address is www.splc.org.

- **The Reporters Committee for Freedom of the Press**. This nonprofit organization provides free legal help to reporters and news organizations. It publishes a variety of materials pertinent to these laws; it also publishes other valuable works on such topics as locating police records, access to states' electronic records, and laws concerning access to public places. For information, contact the Committee at: 1815 N. Ft. Meyer Drive, Suite 900, Arlington, VA 22209; (800) 336-4243. The committee's Web site (www.rcfp.org) also provides valuable resources, including *The First Amendment Handbook*—a great guide to the particulars of privacy, libel, and so on.

About The Center
for Public Integrity

The Center for Public Integrity began operation in May 1990. It is a nonprofit, nonpartisan research organization founded so that important national issues can be investigated and analyzed without the normal time or space limitations. Described as a "watchdog in the corridors of power" by *National Journal*, the Center has investigated and disseminated a wide array of information in nearly forty published Center reports since its inception. More than 3,000 news media stories have referenced the Center's findings or perspectives about public service and ethics-related issues. The Center's books and studies are resources for journalists, academics, and the general public, with databases, backup files of government documents, and other information available as well.

As with its previous books and reports, the views expressed herein do not necessarily reflect the views of individual members of The Center for Public Integrity's Board of Directors or Advisory Board.

For the most recent findings of the Center, including additional or updated information about community activism and investigative journalism (that is to say, muckraking) not contained in this book, you can visit the Center's Web site at www.publicintegrity.org, or sign up for a free online subscription to *The Public i*, the Center's award-winning newsletter (www.public-i.org).

For more information, to buy books and other publications, or to become a member of the Center, contact The Center for Public Integrity:

The Center for Public Integrity
910 Seventeenth Street, N.W.
Seventh Floor
Washington, D.C. 20006

E-mail: contact@publicintegrity.org
Internet: www.publicintegrity.org
Online investigative report: www.public-i.org
Telephone: (202) 466-1300
Facsimile: (202) 466-1101

Acknowledgments

Thanks to Alan Green and Bill Hogan for applying their talents to make this book a reality and to Erin Gallavan for her steadfast research help. Peter Newbatt Smith carefully and tirelessly applied his skillful fact-checking to keep our information accurate and up-to-date. Additional thanks to former staffers Christine Stavem and Alejandro Benes, both of whom had a hand in writing and editing early on, and to William O'Sullivan for his attention to the manuscript. Finally, we owe much gratitude to the Deer Creek Foundation of St. Louis, Missouri, without whose generous support this project would not have been possible.

Index

Index

Index

Index

Index